"Lawyers play a most crucial role in the most sacred task of society, that is, the administration of justice. Hence, they should adhere to the highest ethical standards. Unfortunately, however, as Blaine Nels Simons, a practitioner at the California Bar for approximately 30 years, makes plain in his forthcoming book, GAMES LAWYERS PLAY WITH YOUR MONEY, a small percentage of American lawyers ignore such standards. This book merits the reading of everyone interested in this crucial problem."

Sen. Sam J. Ervin, Jr.

GAMES LAWYERS PLAY WITH YOUR MONEY

BLAINE N. SIMONS

CONDOR

NEW YORK

GAMES LAWYERS PLAY WITH YOUR MONEY

CONDOR

ISBN 0-89516-018-8
Library of Congress Catalog Number: 77-88488

Printed in the United States of America

CONDOR PUBLISHING COMPANY, INC.
521 Fifth Avenue
New York, N.Y. 10017

Dedication

This book is dedicated to that endangered species, the honest lawyer.

Once so abundant that little note was taken of them, honest lawyers are today being ravaged by a cancer within their profession. For centuries this cancer lay benign. It was irritating but controllable. Within the past few years, however, it has become malignant. Spreading slowly but surely through the lawyering profession it may soon—unless radically controlled—destroy the moral tissue of the Law.

The malignancy within the profession is the unethical shyster lawyer. These charlatans are on the march, their numbers rapidly increasing. They are robbing lawyering of the last vestiges of its honesty. They are raping the public not for carnal satisfaction, but for money. They must be stopped.

You, the reader will some day need the services of an attorney. You may be a client now. There are many honest lawyers who will work earnestly in your behalf and charge you fairly. This book will aid you in finding such a lawyer. By learning the money-gouging games of the unethical practitioner you will be steered away from him and into the offices of the reputable attorney. With legal business driven back to the honest lawyer the cancer within the profession will be arrested. The gluttonous shyster who now preys on the public may then disappear. We can only hope so.

ABOUT THE AUTHOR

The author has been engaged in the general practice of law in a West Coast state for the past twenty-eight years. During this period he served two years as a member of the Board of Governors of his local bar association, sixteen years as an officer of the association, and from 1958–76 as editor of its official monthly magazine. He served a five-year term as a member of his state bar's prestigious Family Law Committee, has thrice been a delegate to annual state bar conferences, and has served on numerous committees of his local bar association.

A graduate of the University of Texas Law School, Mr. Simons took his B.A. degree from the University of his home state, South Dakota, and later secured a masters degree in history from Long Beach State College. During World War II he served as a naval officer aboard an LST and took part in the invasion of Normandy.

Married for thirty-two years to a Texas beauty he discovered during World War II, the author is the father of six children ranging in age from thirteen through thirty-one. Semiretired from his law practice due to two heart attacks, Mr. Simons includes among his spare-time ventures teaching evenings at a local junior college and, as he puts it, "spending every minute I can with my children." He is also heavily involved with YMCA work both as a member of its Board of Directors and as a youth group leader.

A long-time advocate of strong bar associations and an opponent of unethical lawyers, the author looks on this book as, hopefully, commencing a new trend in bettering relations between lawyers and the public.

"For generations past," says Mr. Simons, "bar associations have been telling the public that 'lawyers are wonderful guys.' The public doesn't believe it. They read daily of lawyers who have gone astray and equate the doings of these lawyers with all lawyers. There *are* many wonderful guys practicing law— honest, ethical, hardworking ones who toil sixty to eighty hours a week and die at age fifty-seven (the national average), generally of heart attacks.

"Better public relations," he continues, "would be achieved by bar associations spotlighting and ferreting out the shysters in their midst. By telling the public, 'We do have bad guys in our group but we are getting rid of them,' bar associations would be doing the honest lawyer a better service. The public might then believe—as is true—that there are many honest lawyers still around."

TABLE OF CONTENTS

Page

ix

GAMES LAWYERS PLAY WITH YOUR MONEY

CHAPTER 1

Too Many Lawyers

Too many lawyers
Too many tricks,
Too many games with YOUR money!

When, not so long ago that the smell can't be remembered, the fishermen of Congress seined the Watergate Gang from the political seas of Washington, a number of fish caught flopping in their nets were lawyers. Some of these went to jail, some went free, some were disbarred from the practice of law, some were not. Lawyers everywhere were tainted with the fishy smell of their Watergate brethren. As if they needed the publicity!

For centuries lawyers have been trying to clean up their act, spending billions on public relations. Yet, every time a Watergate-type episode hits the headlines, they slip a notch lower in public esteem. Both the Boss Tweed Gang shenanigans of the late nineteenth century and the Teapot Dome scandal of 1923, involved enough lawyers for the public to conclude: "See, every time something crooked occurs there's a lawyer mixed up in it."

Rather than shine the spotlight on the "bad guys," however, lawyers doggedly stick to their archaic public relations theme which announces, "Lawyers are all wonderful guys." Hogwash! A better informed, far more intelligent public than existed a century ago knows better. There *are* a lot of bad guys operating behind "attorney-at-law" shingles.

Worse still, ethics among lawyers are not improving. Yesterday the problem was one of controlling the offenders. It points up the centuries-long problem, when you realize that laws were lax and bar associations had little power. Neither Shakespeare nor Dickens had much good to say about lawyers. Thomas More, writing his *Utopia* in the sixteenth century, decreed that there would be no lawyers in his mythical land of perfection. Lawyers, he wrote, were "a sort of people it is to disguise matters." Then, as now, there were ethical lawyers in the land but their good deeds and hard work were lost in the publicity afforded those of unsavory ethics and little conscience.

The problem today is one of numbers. There are too many lawyers. Although laws requiring high legal ethics are in abundance and although bar associations have great powers to punish today, neither seem able to stem the tide of shaky ethics that is flooding the country today. The situation can be likened to every motorist on every expressway deciding, all at the same time, to travel 110 miles an hour. While the police would catch a few, the vast majority would get away with this transgression.

The key to the games and tricks which an increasing number of lawyers are playing on an unsuspecting public today is the ratio of lawyers to laymen (nonlawyers) in any given area. Attorneys have always considered the ratio of 1 lawyer to every 1000 people as being ideal, 1 to every 750 as being a satisfactory minimum. Out of 750 or 1000 people in the community the lawyer can secure enough legal business to earn a good income. But, as the country continues to be inundated with lawyers the lawyer-to-people ratios are rapidly lowering in every community. Consider the facts:

In 1951 the American Bar Association (hereinafter called the A.B.A.) reported 204,000 lawyers in practice in the United States. The country's population stood at 150 million. The ratio was 735–1.

By 1976 the country's population had increased to some 215 million citizens. By the end of the Bicentennial year it was estimated that 405,000 lawyers would be practicing their art in the nation, putting the ratio at 530–1.

The country's population growth rate was 5 percent between 1970 and 1976. It is likely to continue at this rate, or slightly below it, so that by 1980 the population should stand at about 225 million.

Lawyering, however, is accelerating at a much faster pace. The number of attorneys has doubled in the past twenty-five years while the nation's population has increased at only half that rate. In the period 1970–76, the nation's lawyers increased by almost 50 percent.*

Why is the lawyer/public ratio so important to you, the "buying" public? Simply for this reason: If you, as the present or future client of a lawyer, are to provide his income for him, there must be enough of you to provide it. Should a lawyer's clientele shrink (as it does with lowering ratios) then he must devise other schemes to increase his income or at least to keep it stable. These "other schemes" are easy to come by. You, the public, are bled for a few dollars more, or even thousands more, than would have been the case in better times. If a lawyer earned $75,000 from 300 clients last year, how is he to earn the same amount or more this year with only 150 clients? Doubling his fees is not the perfect answer as many of the 150 would leave him to go elsewhere. Keeping you as a client but playing heretofore secret "games" with your money is the better answer.

You who live in more densely populated areas have more to fear. The small town lawyer remains honest, in the main, because he must cater to the same families

---

*The 405,000 figure was given to me by the A.B.A. It was an estimate on their part and not the result of a survey. My guess is that the figure is closer to 450,000, making a 477–1 ratio of people to lawyers. Assuming the 50 percent rate continues during the next four years (although this rate has accelerated in the past two years) we should have upwards of 675,000 lawyers nationwide by 1980—a ratio of 333–1.

for a lifetime; should he get the reputation of "unethical lawyer" he could be wiped out with nowhere to
go. The big city, big county lawyer, however, can
count on thousands of newcomers pouring into his
area each year. Should his reputation become so
tarnished that his income suffers, he can always move
to another part of the county and set up practice again
with hardly a break in stride.

California provides a good example in point. The
ratio of lawyers to public in the so-called Golden
State—standing at 685–1 in 1950 and 625–1 in 1970—
has now decreased to about 400–1 in six short years.
One thousand new lawyers passed their bar exams in
1960. Eight thousand were admitted to practice as the
result of the 1976 bar exams! Considering 5000 were
admitted in 1975 the percentage of increase is becoming more than a computer can handle. By 1980 the
ratio should be down to 200–1 statewide. In San
Francisco, every 109th person you meet today is a
lawyer in practice. In Los Angeles County the ratio is
364–1 and decreasing rapidly. People in beautiful
Lassen County in the northern California mountains
are luckier. They have but one lawyer for every 2,312
of their population. People living in Alpine County in
the rugged High Sierra are perhaps the luckiest. They
have no lawyers at all!

Like the large cities of California, Honolulu, Seattle
and Miami, have increased their populations primarily
through the influx of outsiders. New York City,
Chicago and Minneapolis have increased theirs
through their birthrate and the big city employment
opportunities they offer suburban householders. All of
these cities, and others, have one thing in common—
lawyers flock to them in droves. Forsaking the lower-
income security of the small town for a chance at the
big stakes available in large metropolitan areas, most
are victims of the "Las Vegas syndrome," the
knowledge that you can win a few bucks in a back
room crap game but you can win a bundle in 'Vegas.
In their pell-mell dash to "where the money's at," few

stop to consider that more people lose than win in the gaming capitals of the world.

Government departments and big business have always been able to absorb a fair share of newly licensed lawyers, but today they cannot keep up with the pace. A spot in the district attorney's office or a new opening with a large corporation may draw over 100 applicants. While many are new lawyers seeking their first foothold on the climb to the top, an increasing number are older lawyers who, feeling the pinch of overwhelming competition, are seeking refuge in a job with a steady income. Those who fail to secure salaried employment return to private practice. There it's individual clients—not the government, not the corporation—who will provide their incomes.

So it is that when you sally forth to retain a lawyer, you may engage either a young one who is desperate for a starting income, or an older one whose income is falling because the people-to-lawyer ratios have decreed that he now will have fewer clients than he did a decade ago. The game is underway. Throughout the encounter these lawyers are on the offensive—trying to part you from your money. You are forever on the defensive, knowing you must of necessity pay out some of your money, but trying to protect yourself against large and unnecessary losses—the "bomb" that is thrown if your defenses are caught napping.

* * *

For most of this book you are in the lawyer's chair looking across the desk at the client. From this perspective you can better understand the tricks, the ruses, the games and devices the lawyer is able to play on his client. You will learn how, through law school training and the experience of practicing law he is able to read your mind, play on your emotions, cater to your strengths, exploit your weaknesses and, in the end, have you eagerly parting with your money as you slide down the legal rainbow toward the pot of gold he has promised will be waiting there. Taxpayers will also find that government attorneys are not past wasting millions of tax dollars annually. They too have games that help them but don't help you, the tax pauper, one iota.

Each chapter outlines what you can do about the particular game the chapter describes. The cure, in a nutshell, is to blow the whistle on unethical lawyers—to bring them to the attention of bar associations, let the public know about them through the newspapers, or, if your case be ripe for it, sue them for malpractice.

Still and all, an ounce of prevention is worth a pound of cure. By understanding the tricks and games that lawyers propose for you in various situations you can prevent these situations from arising. *The money you save is always your own.*

CHAPTER 2

The Good-Case, Bad-Case Game

He has advertised himself as a lawyer, but he is a hypnotist. You have visited him voluntarily, but without you being aware of it, you have been placed in a trance. This particular trance will last as long as your legal matter with this lawyer lasts. Only when you have snapped out of the hypnotic state will your conscious mind tell you that you have been playing a game with a hypnotist.

"What sort of a game?"

"I'm not sure myself."

"Will I ever know *what* game was played?"

"Probably not."

"Did I win or lose?"

"You lost."

Naturally you are going to lose any game in which you are not even aware that you are a participant! The opponent knows all the rules, holds all the cards. What he does is tricky to be sure but more a game than a trick. A trick implies a brief episode. A game may involve many tricks, played over a long period of time. Tricks are often easily recognized. Games are not. They are more subtle.

The Good-Case Game

Every lawyer has the ability to play hypnotic games with his clients. Percentagewise, the numbers engaged in this sport are small, yet, for the reason mentioned in the introduction, their numbers are on the increase.

You, the layman, are about to become a client. You believe in the lawsuit you have brought to the attorney to file. It is your belief that has motivated you to contact an attorney for an appointment.

7

From the moment you walk into the inner sanctum of the lawyer's office he will know he has a potential pigeon. You wouldn't be there if you didn't believe you had a good case. Rare is the man who will pay money to a lawyer to tell him he has a bad case when he, the client, has also come to the same conclusion.

The stage is then set for the first game. You may not be aware that this lawyer is hungry and hurting, eager for any case that comes along. Conversely, his business may be good but he is living beyond his means and constantly needs new cases to feed the gluttony of his personal spending habits. How are you to know?

You relate your story to the attorney. As you talk on he jots down the facts, grunting from time to time, asking questions now and then. As you conclude your statement of the facts, and give your own legal opinion, the lawyer ponders briefly. Then he solemnly advises that "You have a good case here."

The client is pleased. He wanted to verify what he always thought—that he had a good case. Nine out of ten clients visiting a law office to start litigation are convinced they have good cases; the tenth is fairly sure, but wants to be convinced. And it isn't hard to convince a man who wants to hear "yes" that "yes" is the correct answer.

The client may actually have a mediocre case, or even a very bad case, one based on imagined law rather than actual law. An ethical lawyer will tell the client, if this is so. The game-playing lawyer will not. From the client's presentation of his case and from a few questions asked afterwards, the ne'er-do-well lawyer can determine his economic status. He can then set his fees accordingly.

"You have an excellent case, sir," the lawyer advises.

The client beams. He always thought he had.

"But it's a long way from this office to the day of judgment in court," the lawyer continues.

He then outlines everything that could possibly occur between now and the day in court: depositions, written interrogatories, investigations, correspondences and conferences with the other attorney, and legal research. Ah, legal research! He will wave at the many law books in his office. He will intone the truism that a well-prepared case takes hours of legal research. A lawyer sells only one commodity—time. This being the case, all of these matters will cost money.

By now the attorney has sized up the client. He is about to set a fee. What fee he sets will be gauged by three factors: the client's enthusiasm to start the case, the client's apparent financial ability to pay the fee charged, and the end result to be obtained from the case, viz., "What does the client want by way of judgment?" Obviously if the client's goal is $10,000, then only a fool would pay that much by way of fees.

The lawyer will name a retainer ("down payment"). He will watch carefully to see if the client flinches or shows any other signs of the "Gee, that's a lot of money" symptom. Should this happen the lawyer will hasten to say that his fee per hour will be charged against the retainer paid down; that is to say, if the retainer was $1,000, then the client won't owe any more until the lawyer has used that up at the rate of $75 per hour—his standard fee in this example. The still-concerned client will be assured that the fee won't get any larger than the one thousand paid down. If the client relaxes the lawyer may intimate that, by the end of the case, the fee could climb over the one grand mark. How much over is not mentioned. He is the cat, the client is mouse.

If the client does not flinch when the retainer fee is set, our unethical practitioner will then switch tactics. The retainer, he will advise, is just to retain his particular services. He will extol his own virtues in the legal field in which his client's case falls until he is sure the client is convinced. Aside from this first call the client will be charged $75 per hour (or whatever that lawyer is currently charging) for future work. Should the client argue at this point the lawyer can always compromise. Being an expert in this game the lawyer will win it. He will secure the case. Backtracking when needed, speaking in platitudes but always being gracious, he will eventually, if possible, nail down a higher than normal fee.

So he gets a fee. Isn't he entitled to one? Of course he is. But what of the case itself? Was it really a good one? Many "cases" brought to a lawyer's office have serious flaws, some serious enough to make them probable losers if a lawsuit is filed. The lawyer who takes these flaw-filled or downright bad cases after advising "You've got a great case there!" is unethical. The lawyer who charges substantial fees to take losers (without telling the client of the flaws) is dishonest.

Case history A: A couple visited Lawyer Jones for an adoption. An infant child had been left with them by a young couple who stated they would be back in a week. Now, six *months* later they have returned. In the meantime the clients have fallen in love with the baby, but the natural parents have demanded its return. The clients had said "No!" Such was the state of affairs when they visited Lawyer Jones.

"They will not give their consent to our adopting the child and they will fight us if we try to adopt," the woman said.

"But we'll fight 'em all the way," her husband added. "We've got the money."

Jones pointed out the sad law of life to them: that in the state in question the consent of both natural parents was necessary for an adoption to be approved. If the natural parents in fact had abandoned the child, the state could step in and deprive them of the child's custody. The child would then be placed in a duly licensed foster home or, if the natural parents could prove they'd mended their ways, it would be returned to them. The law would not allow his clients to adopt.

Sadder yet, from Jones's point of view, was the fact that the couple was eager to begin proceedings and had $2,000 in cash with them for a retainer. When told they had no case they got mad, not at the law but at Attorney Jones (a common reaction by clients who are told, "You don't have a case"). Telling him he was all wrong they stalked out of the office.

Jones later heard, through the local grapevine, that another lawyer had taken the case. Disbelieving, he called the couple and was told that what he'd heard was true. They smugly advised him that *they* had been right all along; theirs was a good case, Lawyer X told them so. He also got their $2,000 retainer!

Case history B: A young married lady visited Lawyer Smith. She was carrying a Coke bottle. The bottle was her "case." She and her husband had found a quite dead horsefly at the bottom of the bottle. Lawyer Smith, however, noted right off that the bottle was full and, apparently, had never been opened; the cap seemed secure.

"You didn't drink from the bottle?" he inquired.

"Of course not. You can see it's never been opened."

"How did you come to discover the fly?"

"I was about to open the Coke when my husband said he thought something was in the bottom of the bottle. We looked closely and, sure enough, there was this fly."

"What did you do?"

"First we had a good laugh and my husband said I'd better take the bottle back to the store. Then he remembered something."

"What?"

"Well, he said that years ago he'd read where someone had received $10,000 in damages for finding a dead mouse in a Coke bottle. Now, in these times of inflation, he figured a dead horsefly ought to be worth as much."

Lawyer Smith shuddered. He remembered studying the "dead mous " case in law school years ago. He related the facts to his potential client:

"In the mouse case," he advised her, "the person discovered the mouse after the bottle of Coke was almost fully consumed. Looking into the bottle as he was about to take the last gulp, he saw the mouse. The Coke drinker got horribly sick, vomited and went to bed. There were medical expenses incurred for after-care as I recall. A jury, somewhere in the country, gave that person $10,000. The facts in your case are different. You drank no Coke from this bottle—as a matter of fact you never opened it. You laughed and thought it funny when you saw the horsefly. You were not damaged in any way."

He went on to point out that the most she could expect was a refund on the bottle or, if a claim was filed, perhaps a nuisance-value settlement not amounting to much.

He promptly lost a client, but maintained good ethics. Later Lawyer Smith must have smarted when he learned that another local attorney had taken a fly in a Coke bottle case. The lady described sounded like the one Smith had seen in his office. The exceptions were, however, that when she arrived at the new lawyer's office the bottle was almost empty and she had a gory story to tell about vomiting and nausea resulting from her seeing the fly just as she was polishing off the last dregs of the Coke. Smith was furious. He had set her up. Learning how people secured damages for mice and flies in Coke bottles, she had presented another version of the facts. She later got some sort of settlement—and rather more than "nuisance value" suggests.

Case history C: A prospective client was involved in an "uncontrolled intersection" accident. There were no stop signs, no stop and go signals, no witnesses, no police report. Each driver claimed he had entered the intersection first—the old "one person's word against another's" situation. Both cars sustained great physical damage, an indication to the listening lawyer that both may well have been exceeding the fifteen mile an hour speed limit at that intersection. The would-be client had sustained grievous bodily injuries, as had the driver of the other auto.

Since he had been injured the client felt he was entitled to damages. The lawyer told him the truth, namely that to recover damages in a personal injury case there must be three salient features: financial responsibility (the other car must be insured or its driver own assets capable of sustaining payment of a judgment), liability ("fault"), and injuries. Injuries he had, and the other car was insured. Yet, explained the lawyer, the liability was unclear. To prevail in the courts of that state the client must prove he did not contribute to the cause of the accident by being negligent himself, and must also be able to sustain the burden of proof by having a preponderance of the evidence (the "hair over 50 percent"—the 50.0000001 percent proof) leaning in his favor. Because of the complexity of the case the lawyer turned it down. He added that he would take it as a straight fee case but that he would recommend against it because the fee would probably run over $1,000 and the client was quite likely to lose the case.

By "shopping around" the client eventually found a lawyer who told him straight off that he had a great case but who also told him that, in his opinion, contingent fees were unethical (which they were not) and thus got the client to agree to a good cash fee contract.

The sad feature of all of these "Gee, you've got a good case" matters (when the opposite is true and is known to be true by the lawyer), is that in the end the client will lose. But the unscrupulous lawyer has a good alibi. He can blame it on the judge or jury and walk away. It is they who let the client down. Appeal? Sure, but that will be another $5,000. The client, while unhappy, knows the lawyer did his best. Didn't he see the lawyer take extensive depositions, pound the counsel table in court, recite from cases that favored the client's position, *ad infinitum* (and ad nauseam), and give a brilliant closing argument to the jury?

The game involved is really one of mind reading. The attorney can read the client's mind. He knows the client is eager to file suit and, feewise, he can determine how much the traffic will bear. The client, on the other hand, being inexperienced in these matters, cannot read the lawyer's mind. The lawyer's mind has concluded the case is a bad one, or fair at most, but this opinion doesn't show on his face. On the contrary, the client sees only that the lawyer is obviously excited about taking such a good case.

The Bad-Case Game

A variation to the "Gee, you've got a good case" game, is the lawyer's early knowledge that the case *is* a good one. Yet he should not be over eager, for the client may well say, "Why should your fee be so high if the case if such a good one?" In these situations the unethical lawyer will resort to the "bad-case game."

The gambit used in this game is for the lawyer to gently but firmly downgrade the client's case. It isn't really as good as the client believes it to be. There are many legal flaws, many factual gaps which the client, as a nonlawyer, had not considered. The prospective client is then led backwards, as it were, from a good case position to one where he feels his case maybe isn't so good after all. When he feels the client-to-be is ready for it the lawyer springs the trap:

"But I'll take the case."

"I thought you said it was a bad case."

"Not a *bad* case, sir—just not quite as good as you believed it to be."

The lawyer goes on to explain that he enjoys challenging cases, that he specializes in winning cases that, in the beginning, didn't look so good. He is sure that he, of all the lawyers in town, can win it. He also adds that he likes the client, a person whom he knows has suffered much, and who has good moral cause for finding restitution through the courts. With this added note of flattery to bolster his waning spirits, the client is ready to discuss fees.

If the case is one in which a contingent fee would normally be charged (e.g. a personal injury case), the fee might be higher than an ethical lawyer would charge (because, after all, the case isn't too good and the lawyer must do a lot of extra work to make it a winner) or he might take some cash plus a smaller percentage. Client takes the bait.

In the straight cash fee case the lawyer is now in a position to quote a higher fee. Again, he is taking a sow's ear and, through hard work, almost guaranteeing he will make it into a silk purse. This the client understands and pays up accordingly.

The bad-case game is, once again, a matter of mind reading. The lawyer knows the case is a good one but the words he speaks give no sign that it is. The client's mind is easily read: he knows he has a good case and wants to file suit.

The net result of the good-case, bad-case games is an over-charge to the client. In addition, in the good-case game, where a bad case is taken and charged for on the pretense that it's a good case, the client is roundly bilked. Through training and experience the lawyer knows such a case has little chance of winning but leads the client to believe the opposite is true. After the initial interview plus, if needed, some investigation and legal research, the lawyer should know whether the client's case is good, bad or middling. He is then duty bound to give the client his opinion. If he is unsure even after interview, investigation and research, he will seek the advice of some attorney friend who specializes in this particular field of law. He should then level with the client, tell him the truth about the case.

What you can do about the Good-Case, Bad-Case game

1. Know something about the lawyer you visit professionally. It is surprising the number of people who select a lawyer by the hit-or-miss method.

Every year a few of the people who visit me tell me, in answer to my query, that they were referred to me by the yellow pages of their phone directory. The yellow pages are fine, but until 1977 lawyers could only list their names there. Now that lawyers can advertise in the yellow pages (see Chapter on "Advertising," infra), you may learn something more about them, i.e. what they want to tell you about themselves. Remember, however, Lawyer X may *claim* to be a specialist in every branch of law, but how can you be sure that he is?

"How did you come to pick my name out of the 500 or more attorney names in our local listings?" I would always inquire in the pre-advertising days.

Some liked my first name, some my last, some the "sound" of my whole name ("It has a nice ring to it"); some picked me because they had known people with the same first name as mine. What a way to choose a lawyer!

Every lawyer must get an average of at least two calls a year as the result of people picking his name at random from lists of lawyers—stark lists with no indication of his field of special expertise. This means that nearly a million people a year seek a lawyer through the list-of-names method.

"Walk-ins" are also a constant source of business for many lawyers. A client-to-be sees an attorney's name on an office window or "shingle." Remembering that he wants to see a lawyer, he walks in. Some of legal history's biggest cases have just "walked in." Of these clients some get a good lawyer, some don't. Some get a specialist in the field appropriate to their case, some don't. Those making out all right through the use of this method are—like those who pick from a list—just plain lucky. They could, and should, have made a few inquiries before selecting an attorney. How do you do this?

A. *Check with your local bar association.* Most of these associations have lists of lawyers in your area who specialize in certain fields of law. An attorney specializing in the field of law into which your case falls is the lawyer you want. Bar associations are always trying to improve the public's image of lawyers. They won't knowingly steer you to a bad attorney. Should you have a bad experience with a lawyer to whom they refer you, make certain you report this back to the association. Your complaint may help others in the future. It will also go a long way toward getting *that* lawyer to shape up or ship out!

B. *Check with friends and neighbors.* Someone in this category must have had experiences with attorneys who have handled legal matters for them. Get a list of several such attorneys. If the experience with that attorney was a good one, give him a plus sign. A plus also goes for the attorney who handles cases in the field into which your matter falls. Take some time over this selection process for it substantially increases your chances of finding an honest, capable professional.

The vast majority of lawyers' business comes from satisfied "customers." A happy client will refer others, and that's how a solid law practice is built. Needless to say if your friend or neighbor raves about Lawyer A, there's something to A worth recommending. When you visit him tell him immediately who it was who referred you to him. Noting that you were referred by a satisfied client, the lawyer will bend over backwards to ensure that you become another satisfied client.

2. Shop around. Many people will shop days for "just the right car" and hours for clothing, but they will walk into a lawyer's office blind and sign up without any checking around whatsoever. Once inside the door, few leave unsigned.

Unless you are absolutely, 100 percent satisfied with the first lawyer you see, and unless he was highly recommended, visit several lawyers for the purpose of discussing your case. You can decide later which one of them to choose. Take notes as he talks. What are his fee charges? How long has he been in practice? (Plaques on his wall can give you this answer.) What are his personal, honest-to-God thoughts about your case? Finally, and perhaps most importantly, how did you get on with him personally? Many lawyer/client contracts dissolve along the way because of a clash of personalities. Pick out a lawyer with whom you feel comfortable. He must be someone you can trust. An attorney who seems wise enough but whom you don't like will soon sow seeds of distrust within you. Some like lawyers who are as comfortable as an old shoe, others like the unsmiling, all-business type. Others prefer lawyers who have gained some local or national fame (this allows the client to bathe vicariously in this spotlight of fame); they feel that if the lawyer is famous he must be good. This is sometimes a correct assumption, but not always.

If you are "shopping around," however, it is only fair that you tell this to the lawyer ahead of time. As previously stated, lawyers sell only one commodity, *time*, and being frank with the lawyer may save you a bill for the interview. On being advised that he is only one of several you will be visiting, the attorney should then advise you:

(a) whether he will confer with you "on speculation," viz., in hopes of getting your case but not charging for the interview if he does not, or

(b) whether he will bill you for the conference anyway.

If you get the latter advice you can always leave; but if you stay, that is, start paying for time, get to the point of your case with dispatch. If the attorney charges for the interview, determine if this fee will be a part of the final fee he will charge if you give him your case.

Clients who level with attorneys at the outset of an interview almost invariably get better results in regard to both time and money spent. If you want your attorney to be frank with you, you must be frank with him.

3. Shy away from the lawyer who is overly enthusiastic about your legal matter and can't wait to sign you up. Beat a hasty retreat from the lawyer who bad-

mouths your case but then wants to sign you up anyway, offering all sorts of deals to get you to affix your signature to the attorney contract. Such lawyers may well be playing the "good-case, bad-case game." In such cases you lose, they win!

CHAPTER 3

Zeroing in on the Bank Account

If you were given access to a $50,000 bank account and advised that you could legally have as much of it as you wanted, the probabilities are that you would take the entire amount. Why not? Human instinct decrees that, within the bounds of law and morality, we should take all we can get.

Lawyers have human instincts too. Their instincts, however, are governed by Codes of Ethics under which they must practice. These codes (state laws) set forth what attorneys can and cannot do in their relationships with clients, the public in general and the courts. The overriding theme of every such code as it concerns the attorney/client relationship, is that the lawyer is not to take undue advantage of the client. The majority of attorneys don't. An ever-increasing minority, however, do take this advantage when they have the chance. We saw this in the "good-case, bad-case" situation. There it was a matter of not revealing to the client that he had a very good case (the "bad-case game") or that he had a bad case (the "good-case game").

Zeroing in on a client's bank account is probably the most prevalent of lawyer games. Its popularity is on the rise, and *you* are the victim. Why should you have all that money when your lawyer needs it? Here the game is not predicated on how good or bad your case is (though many a bad case is taken so that the attorney can get to your bank account), but rather on how much money you have in the bank. The shyster's primary concern is to get to that account for fees, fees and more fees.

Once the case has been accepted, the unethical attorney will begin devising ways to get the money in your account over into his. Although this can be done in a great variety of cases, the game lends itself especially well to actions for divorce. Across the length and breadth of our land there are more divorce cases filed than any other single kind. In them there is an endless number of tasks that can be undertaken by the lawyer—pleadings, depositions, interrogatories, motions, preliminary hearings of many sorts, conferences, correspondence and the inevitable daily telephone calls to or from the client. Obtaining the client's consent to these work items is comparatively easy in most instances. The fire was lit when the case was started. The parties disliked each other enough to start the proceedings. All the lawyer must do is fan the flames, making certain the fire remains ablaze until:

    (a) the case is over, or

    (b) the parties run out of money. The fire he must fan involves every negative emotion in the human spectrum: hate, avarice, revenge, greed, bitterness, anger, fear, rancor. You name it, it's there in the divorce case. All the lawyer must do is toss a word in now and then to keep the flames high. If the parties seem inclined toward settlement or reconciliation, a stern lecture by the greedy attorney may be needed to turn a party back on the road posted "Fight On!" Well trained in the art of doing this, the lawyer can take even the simplest of cases and turn it into a donnybrook.

Example: As divorce cases go, the matter of *Sueyou vs. Sueyou* was a simple one. The case was one which would lend itself to easy settlement. Wife would get the family home, husband his pension rights; the values of the two equalled out almost to the dollar. The only thing else they had was one large bank account. Bank accounts are easy to divide: split 'em down the middle. In the county where this case arose, the domestic relations court had a "support table" which provided guidelines for judges in the setting of temporary and final child support and alimony: no problem.

But there *was* a problem. The amount in the Sue-yous' bank account was $25,000. The lawyer whom the wife saw in order to begin the divorce action noticed it right away. A bright young lawyer with his eyes on that golden egg, his failing was that he wasn't earning enough as yet to live as he would like to live. His clientele was not large enough to support his monetary appetite, he still had to hustle for a buck. How to get at that $25,000, *that* was the question.

Noting that the wife wasn't working and that she didn't plan to work (the couple had one child, age fifteen), the attorney suggested right off that $750 per month would be a fair figure for support for herself and the child. She was delighted, especially since her husband was only making $950 per month. (The county "table" for temporary support for a wife and one child on this income was $425 per month but the lawyer didn't mention this.)

The husband was aghast when he found that his wife wanted to leave him only $200 per month to live on and to kick him out of the house as well. He saw his own lawyer. A settlement proposal was made by the husband's attorney, with support in line with the county's proposed tables, to be reduced a year later when, it was presumed, the wife would find employment.

The reply to the settlement proposal was "divorce papers" served on the husband. In these the wife now asked for more than fifty percent of the parties' property (in that state the law required it be divided up fifty-fifty). The husband was livid. No amount of explaining to him that the court would, eventually, give him half could assuage his anger.

The wife in turn had papers served on the husband for a preliminary hearing to determine temporary support and to have him removed from the home. At the hearing she stated she needed $790 by way of support (but would take $750). The husband showed estimated expenses for himself of $700 should he be ordered to leave the home.* The court was then left with the problem of squeezing the $1450 the couple needed out of the $950 in total income, which of course it couldn't do. Because the husband had no history of violence toward his wife, he was allowed to remain in the family home (in a separate bedroom) pending the divorce hearing itself.

Now the wife was livid! Her lawyer had a truly "contested case" on his hands. If either party had been in a settling mood earlier they were no longer. Anger had replaced reason, and "Fight On!" was the battle cry.

Eyeing the bank account and taking a deep breath, the wife's attorney thereupon proceeded to serve a "boilerplate" set of Written Interrogatories on the husband's attorney. As earlier mentioned, inter-rogatories are written questions which the husband must answer in writing and under oath. Going through the questions and rough-drafting the answers is a laborious procedure for a party and his/her attorney. This work, together with typing up the final answers, takes plenty of time. Since time is what a lawyer sells, the fees start their upward climb.

"Boilerplate" interrogatories are a stock set of questions which many lawyers draw up by the thousands of pages. Each set may run from 25 to 100 pages or more, with questions sometimes numbering into the many hundreds. They are called "boilerplate" not only because they are thick, but because they cover every possible question that could arise in any divorce case. In the average, run-of-the-mill case, per-

---

*A husband living alone will often spend as much as a wife and several children living in the family home. Apartment rentals are generally higher than house payments. With no kitchen facilities he will eat his meals out, which is more expensive than eating at home. His clothes, auto expenses and family bills incurred in the past, and still owing, run his totals up considerably more than most would expect.

haps 80 percent of the questions are totally irrelevant.
The lawyer served with such papers can either:

(a) go to court on a formal motion to have the irrelevant questions stricken, or

(b) go ahead and answer them anyway.

Since making the motion and the court appearance involved will both cost the client money, the ethical lawyer will often weigh the relative cost to the client before deciding which route should be taken. Often it is cheaper to answer the questions. In any event, the matter is always discussed with the client. (or *should* be). If some of the irrelevant questions stumble into ground the party does not wish the opposition to discover, there may be a motion for the quashing of these questions, involving more attorney fees.

In the case we are discussing, the wife's lawyer may have had this in mind because several of his more irrelevant questions fell in subject areas the husband did not particularly want to discuss. Others were so irrelevant as either to make the husband laugh or make him angry over such time-wasting nonsense. One of the few questions that seemed relevant to me made the husband more than a little upset:

149. List the stocks and bonds you own, either in your name alone, with your wife, or with others, including:

    A. Date of purchase;

    B. Purchase price;

    C. From whom acquired;

       (and so on, down to sub-question M)

What upset the husband was that he not only owned no stocks or bonds, as his wife of twenty years knew, but that he hated stocks and bonds with a vengeance, as she also knew. His wife knew that his family had been wiped out in the stock-market crash of '29 and that he'd been raised as a child to hate the stock market.

"The gall of my wife to ask a question like that," he

shouted. "I'll guarantee she did it just to make me mad."

It was her lawyer, of course, and not the wife who had asked the question. He had simply told his secretary to "put together a divorce case boilerplate" and had it mailed out.

Husband and lawyer finally put together the answers to some 200 questions posed, including a capitalized NO to the query as to whether this Iowa-born-and-raised man (whose wife was from the same town) was an illegal alien.

Now for the "kicker." Should the husband serve a set of interrogatories on his wife? An ethical lawyer will recommend a yes answer to this question, the reason being that since the wife found out, through her interrogatories, what the husband would testify to in court, he should likewise determine in advance what her testimony should be. The honest attorney's method of doing this would be to go through the file and pose in the husband's interrogatories completely relevant questions having to do with the facts and issues of *this* case. From a client's point of view this is definitely less expensive. It is also a great aid to the trial judge because, to render a proper judgment, he must zero in on the important issues of the case.

In the Sueyou case the husband's attorney recommended the shorter, relevant, to-the-point interrogatories.

"Not on your tin-type!" bellowed the husband. "She asked me all these fool questions. You ask her the same questions right back again."

Out goes a "boilerplate" to the wife's attorney and up go the fees again. The initial lawyer, zeroing in on the bank account, is also making a better fee for his opposing lawyer. With twenty-five "thou" to work with, there's money enough for all!

Depositions follow—to clear up points raised by answers to interrogatories or to explore new fields perhaps opened up by the interrogatories. Depositions are oral and taken before court-certified reporters. They get fees too. Lawyers make additional fees in preparing for and appearing at the depositions. That bank account is being slowly eaten away.

There are written settlement proposals between the lawyers' offices or other correspondence, conferences now and again with the client—more fees at every turn.

The case is set for trial. It is continued (postponed) by the court when, by noon, it is obvious no courtroom is available to hear the case, meaning more fees for the lawyers. The second time around it happens again. In his heart each lawyer knew it would because in that particular courthouse a divorce case has the chance of a snowball in hell of getting to trial before the fourth or fifth time around. The wife's lawyer is stunned the third time the case is set when, saints preserve us, the case is sent for trial!

The trial lasts the better part of a day. The judge's decision, handed down two weeks later, gave the husband his pension fund, the wife the home; what was left in the bank was to be split fifty-fifty by the parties. Permanent child support and alimony were set at a figure lower than that which had been granted as temporary support. Sound familiar? Of course, it's what the parties could have, would have, should have settled for at the outset. How much did the parties pay out in attorney fees, court costs and appraiser's fees from their $25,000 bank account? Answer: $10,000 and change.

Such is life when one lawyer, and sometimes two decide to zero in on a bank account.

* * *

While the divorce case provides the best opportunity for a zeroing-in job, it by no means provides the only one. A lawyer playing the good-case, bad-case game may have talked the client into proceeding with a case because he found a large bank account available for fees. Lines between the games are easily crossed and the unethical lawyer may be playing several games at the same time. The insidious part of the game is always that the client never knows he's involved in a game and the lawyer will never admit the fact even at game's end. Everything he did, every service he performed, was "legal" and, albeit in almost every instance he could have achieved the same result with less work, it can never be proved that he did more work than "necessary."

A large bank account is not always the necessary ingredient in this game. The game can be played in a volume-type business with the lawyer zeroing in on what little a number of clients may have. A Los Angeles attorney was recently found to be charging a large Mexican clientele anywhere from thirty dollars to seventy-five dollars for services he then failed to perform. The sum doesn't sound like much but when multiplied by 1,000 and more, the figure reached is high. This shades into the "getting all the traffic will bear" game (which is played primarily by criminal law lawyers and will be discussed later).

Any client with a lousy case but solid monetary assets has a good chance of becoming the victim of the zeroing-in game. The attorney will rush into battle, picking up fees left and right for this and that until at case's end the "fall guys"—the judge or jury ruling against the client—will get the blame. It wasn't the lawyer's fault they lost! In any case, the client's bank account will be considerably less when the case is closed.

What You Can do About the Zeroing-in-on-the-bank-account Game

1. The first step is the selection of a good (ethical) lawyer in accordance with the guidelines set forth at

the conclusion of the "good-case, bad-case game" discussion.

2. No lawyer, despite cries to the contrary, is above suspicion when a great deal of money is involved. The most honest answer ever given by a lawyer involved the question:

"Would you be tempted by a million dollars in your trust account (client's money) or by the fact that your client had a million to spend on fees?"

Answer: I honestly don't know. I've never had a client with near that much money, nor have I ever had more than a couple of thousand in my trust account. I like to believe I wouldn't be tempted."

How does the client, facing his new lawyer across the desk, know what financial predicaments that lawyer might be in right now? The wealthy-looking lawyer with rich and modern offices may need money more than the run-of-the-mill attorney. The very young lawyer may be dying for a dollar and unable to resist the temptation to meet a mortgage, office overheads or other expenses by zeroing in on the thousands the new client may have available for fees. The most honest lawyer on the face of the earth may at this one particular moment in his life need money. Much as he may dislike doing it, and much as it may go against his better judgment, he may zero in to get the fee that will pull him out of his difficulties.

Overcoming the zeroing-in problem is not a simple task. The best advice is to *constantly keep track of what your lawyer is doing on your case* and with your money.

a) Ask for itemized monthly statements. You are entitled to them in straight fee cases. Check these statements carefully each month. Keep them all. In checking back later you may find that some items (inadvertently or otherwise) have been billed more than once. If you have questions concerning any of the billed items, contact the lawyer. You are entitled to an answer. You're his "boss" as much as the employer for whom you work is your boss. If he dodges contact with you or, on contact, doesn't give straight-arrow answers, you can always change attorneys. There's no law against it.

b) Question any work your attorney is doing for you that you feel may be unnecessary. Those persons involved in divorces should be especially careful to put reason ahead of bitterness. Why are depositions needed in a simple issue case? Why is a second four-way conference necessary (two parties, two lawyers) when the first conference fizzled and both lawyers got good fees for it? Why all this correspondence with opposing counsel when nothing is coming of it? Why? Why? Don't be afraid to ask questions.

c) Come up with what you consider a fair-to-all settlement offer early in the proceedings. Make certain your attorney communicates it to the other side; if he hears nothing, have him make the offer again. It stands to reason that if you are interested in taking a settlement offer but your attorney wants to hold out for more, you should do what your mind tells you, not (in this instance) what the attorney tells you. Attorneys too often, far too often, interject themselves into the proceedings as though it was their money, their property, and their own hides that comprised the subject under discussion for settlement. They are on ego trips! If you and the other party are satisfied the settlement is fair, take it. Whether the attorney feels it is fair is both immaterial and irrelevant. He is your agent at law, *you* are the principal; you, not he, must decide what is fair. Should he keep pressing you to go on with the suit, he may well be still zeroing in on your bank account. After all, why should he stop the suit now and settle if you still have more money to spend on fees?

d) Aside from cases such as divorce or accountings, where what you have in property and money are issues, there is no need to reveal to your attorney what you have in the bank, or in stocks, bonds or realty. Outside of a few types of cases, it is none of his business.

The way you appear to your attorney has a bearing on the fees he will charge. If you park a big Cadillac in front of his office, dress fit to kill, and talk about how wealthy you are, the attorney can jump to an easy conclusion: you've got money. Impress others, not your attorney. Your case, not your material wealth, is what should count. One of the richest men I've ever known dressed like a bum at all times. He was the client of an associate of mine and I often felt sorry for him until I learned he was worth a solid two million dollars. When, as an out-of-stater, I was taking my law school training in Texas, I noticed that during the business day rich people tended to dress like poor people, whereas the poorer people were, the better dressed they tended to be. Only in the evening, when they were consorting socially with their own kind, did the rich folks run out their Caddies, put on their white ties and brush off their tails. Don't give your lawyer the wrong impression unless it's to lead him to believe you're just the average citizen. Otherwise, who knows, he might zero in on your bank account whether you have one or not!

CHAPTER 4

Criminal Law Games

Lawyers specializing in criminal law matters make more money, year in and year out, than lawyers in any other field of endeavor. If confronted with this statement, criminal lawyers would cry in unison, "No, no, 'tain't true!" They would point quivering forefingers at the fancy corporate lawyer or the probate attorney and claim that *they* are the big money-makers. "Our clients are mostly poor folk," they would moan—and indeed these clients *are* a good deal poorer when their criminal law cases have been concluded. Criminal law specialists will deny to the end that they make good money. Most wish to appear as poor and humble practitioners. The unethical ones have another reason for their fervent denials of huge incomes: they don't want Uncle Sam to find out.

The average lawyer will tell you that the only way to make money as a lawyer is to marry it or inherit it. For most of them there is much truth in the statement, though they may all get a criminal law case now and then. In that event, the shyster can make a few extra dollars by playing the "criminal law games." Only the specialist in the field, however, can get rich through these unethical practices.

There are several games the lawyer may play in the criminal law field. As a preface to discussing these it should be remembered that the criminal lawyer always knows:

(a) the criminal laws of his state, and

(b) the policies of local courts, both federal and state, as to the disposition of various criminal matters.

The easiest example would be to compare the outcome of a case involving a first-offender charged with petty theft (e.g., shoplifting), with one involving a man accused of grand theft whose list of prior convictions runs two pages long (single spaced). It is obvious that, on a plea of guilty, the former would get a lighter sentence than the latter. A well-trained criminal lawyer can usually predict, almost with certainty, what his client may expect should he plead guilty. The lawyer will also know the current policies of the district attorney or local prosecutor that could help or hinder his clients' cases in various fields. Trying jury cases quite often, as he does, he will soon get to know the mental make-up of the current panel of jurors sitting in the local courts; some panels are tough, some lenient. With this store of information he can usually help his client over the criminal court traces but, at the same time, can fatten his wallet if he chooses to play games.

a) The Misdemeanor Game

Black's Law Dictionary defines a "misdemeanor" as:

> "Any crime which is neither punishable by
> death or by imprisonment in a state prison."

The public knows misdemeanors as "little crimes" and felonies as "biggies". A schoolchild knows that running a red traffic light in your auto is a misdemeanor while murder is a felony. Following Black's definition, however, American states distinguish the two by *where* the guilty person will be incarcerated (prison or jail) and *how long* the term of sentence will be (e.g., one year maximum in jail will be a misdemeanor, one year or more in prison a felony.) What is a misdemeanor in one state may be a felony in another, and vice versa. The criminal lawyer, steeped in criminal-code book learning, will know the difference.

Unfortunately for the public, however, there is more than jail time involved in misdemeanors. There are fines, loss of drivers' licenses, special programs the guilty person must attend or become involved in, restitution to the victim of property destroyed or stolen and a myriad "little things" that members of the public accused of misdemeanors will not know about until they see their lawyers. Even the smallest cases can have harsh results, as, for example, when a truck driver loses his driver's license.

During his first interview the games-playing criminal lawyer can size up his client personally while sizing up the case in hand. While he will play the "fear game" to some extent in misdemeanors, or even hammer away at this game in the case of the truck driver standing to lose his license, his primary game in the misdemeanor field is the "How much will the traffic bear?" game. The game is much akin to the "zeroing-in-on-the-bank-account" gambit discussed earlier. Here, however, rather than having a case that might drag on and on until the bank account is exhausted, the lawyer has a quick-time matter before him. Criminal cases are given preference in getting to trial and the areas of extra work are far more limited than in, say, the divorce field. The criminal lawyer must then fall back on "How much will the traffic bear?" for this particular criminal case.

The traffic-will-bear game has many aspects. The simplest is that the attorney, discovering the client to be well off, will simply double or triple what his ordinary fee would be for the ordinary guy. He will mention the figure without batting an eye. The client, accustomed to big money, will pay. What might have been a $500 case becomes a $1500 case.

Should the client not bat an eye when the fee is set, and start reaching for his wallet, a further dialogue might ensue:

Lawyer: "That fee, of course, is assuming we plead guilty after making a deal with the D.A. If we can't make a deal we may have to go to trial."

Client: "How much more will that be?"

"Lawyer: "I would estimate the trial at a week. My fees run $500 per day."

Client: "That's $3,500!"

Lawyer (quickly): "Five-day court week—$2,500.

[But having noted some panic in the client] for *you* only another $1,500—*if* we go.''

Client: "Fine," (or, slowly) "Sounds a little high but it's okay.''

The games-playing lawyer, already about to earn more by thrice than he would on the same case in an average set of circumstances, can let it go at that or come down some more. He will play it by ear, learning how much the traffic will bear—how far to go, when to retract, when to stop.

Should the client show fear, even though the charge may be a misdemeanor, the attorney may combine the "fear game" to secure a heavier traffic in fees. While the fear game is the primary sport in felony matters and will be discussed later, it is enough here to say that the miscreant in a minor matter may still fear the consequences of his act: the loss of his driver's license, public shame if word of his misdeed is leaked to the public, jail time resulting in the loss of a good job, and a variety of other things. Several times during the initial interview the client will mention these fears. The games-playing attorney will then know he has enough ammunition to play the all-the-traffic-will-bear game even though the client is of modest circumstances. The ethical attorney, on the other hand, will seek to assuage his client's fears; knowing local policy for various crimes he can pretty well tell the client what to expect and, nine times out of ten, the fears of the misdemeanant will not be realized.

The unethical attorney will point out that, yes, the client does stand to lose his driver's license in such matters as drunk or reckless driving. He will not pass on to the client the information that in the local courts, on a first such offense (and often even on a second or third offense), the court does not take away a man's license. He lets the client's fears remain. He then names a higher than usual fee. What constitutes "higher than usual" will vary from town to town and state to state, but since a simple case is now going to be made a difficult case the fee will naturally be higher.

Client: "Gee, that's a pretty steep fee."

Lawyer: "Admittedly, sir. But the thing is: *I am going to save your driver's license for you!*"

Client: "You really can?"

Lawyer: "Yes I can. But it's going to take conferences with the prosecuting attorney and maybe even the judge. I've been around a long time. They know me. They even owe me a few favors."

Client: "How can I pay such a fee? I don't have that kind of money in the bank."

Lawyer: "We'll work that out. A note putting up your home or car as security is the general method. Many do it. It's worth it, too—to save your license and maybe your job—isn't it?"

And so the client pays and, sure enough, a deal is worked out. After he pleads guilty he hears the judge say there will be no suspension of his license and that the fine may be paid out in installments. The attorney did a great job, as promised. Of course what the client doesn't know is that all of this would have happened anyway. The judge was just following long-established local policy.

If the misdemeanor involved is one concerning morals, the client may not want his family to find out about it. If they already know, he may still want to keep the information from the general public. Being found working in, or patronizing a house of prostitution is a case in point. "Morals," however, vary from area to area. What may be a felony in one state may be a misdemeanor in another. In some jurisdictions such offenses can, from the patron's point of view, be changed to simple "disturbing the peace" charges (an apt play on words) or the plea and sentencing can be done in the judge's chambers. The lawyer playing games would not so advise the client, however, and playing on his fears would extract what the traffic would bear in fees before proceeding.* The prostitute-client generally pays extra for having the lawyer get the matter set late in the afternoon, or early in the morning before regular calendar call, so that she can get in and out of court with little or no publicity. On the first or second arrest she generally pays more to the lawyer, on a fee per hour basis, than his average client would. By the third or fourth time the prostitute has learned the game and will either handle her own case or get down to brass tacks with her lawyer, telling him she understands the game and doesn't want to pay out the kind of money she's been paying in the past. The game players earn more from the first- and second-time offenders than from those who make a career out of going to court as defendants; the latter group know the "games" by then and the attorney can't kid them into believing he has a lot more work to do than he really has.

There are, of course, far more misdemeanors committed each year than felonies. The experienced criminal law practitioner, knowing this, realizes that the bulk of his cases will be the former. After a period of time in the business he becomes an expert in finding out just how much the traffic will bear when these cases confront him. He listens not only to what the client is saying but also learns from his demeanor, facial expressions and overall attitude just how far he can go with him. By the time the fee is mentioned he knows the client's job and social position in the community as well. He knows enough about the client by

----

*Prostitution has always been a crime and generally a misdemeanor. Historically, persons found patronizing houses of ill fame (men) were not charged with criminal activity. Thanks to the pressure of modern women's rights movements, however, this is slowly but surely changing. Now, in many jurisdictions, patrons picked up in raids are also charged with misdemeanors. "What's wrong for the goose," say these laws, "is wrong for the gander too."

now to name a fee that will not drive him from the office.* The fee he names might even be a bit higher than he feels he should charge; this is done so that he can cut back if the client protests.

What you can do about the chief misdemeanor game: "How much will the traffic bear?"

1. On your first visit to the attorney zero in on him before he gets the chance to zero in on you. Intimidate, rather than be intimidated. Go immediately to the one thing he may have been going to use later to surprise you: the exact wording of the section of the Code you are charged with violating. Be prepared for a pretty tough-sounding offense. As soon as the attorney has completed the reading of the law you are alleged to have violated, ask him what local policy is in these matters. In Long Beach, California, for example, the attorney might have read from Vehicle Code Section 23102 wherein a first drunk driving offense can get the offender one to six months in jail and/or $250 to $500 in fines. The ethical lawyer will tell the client, however, that in the local courts on first offenses (1975) the courts rarely, if ever, impose jail time, that the fine is only a bit over $300 and that arrangements can be made to pay the fine a week or a month later, or in installments. The judges very, very rarely pull a driver's license on a first offense.

The unethical lawyer might say that every case is different and that he cannot predict in advance the outcome of your case. Don't let him kid you. Particularly on first offenses, most jurisdictions have established

---

*Lawyers will sometimes be presented with a case they don't want and, rather than turn it down, name a fee so high that they know the client won't take it. One lawyer of my acquaintance has twice done this but with the client accepting the fee even though the lawyer advised him he could get the work done more cheaply elsewhere.

sentencing policies. If he hems and haws or insists certain terrible things may happen to you (e.g., a $500 fine, six months in jail and the loss of your license as in the Section 23102 just cited), it's best you move on to another lawyer. This one wants to play games with your money.

2. Neither by word nor expression show any fear of the courtroom consequences of your charge. You have established immediately that this is a misdemeanor and being a first offender (often if you are a *second* offender), you have little to fear in today's judicial world of fines and probation.

3. Get down to brass tacks on the fee as soon as you have explained the circumstances leading to your arrest. Whether you make $2,000 a month, or only $500, should have no bearing on the fee. A rich man who breaks a plate-glass window and steals a record album should pay no more than the modest-income individual who does the very same thing. The complications of the case, not the wealth of the person charged, should be the criteria for the fee charge. Never forget that a lawyer sells one thing and one thing only: *time*.

4. Again, select your lawyer through a friend who has had a good experience in legal matters with him, or through your local bar association. The present trend is to allow lawyers to advertise their specializations. Pick one with a criminal law specialty. Let him know right off that you were referred to him by the local bar association. Then, if you feel he isn't dealing fairly with you, you can report the fact to the association. Chances are that, knowing you were referred by the association, he will think twice about playing games with you. He may get a considerable amount of business through his association and lawyers don't like to kill a goose that is laying golden eggs.

5. You should be frank with your attorney at all times. If you have had prior convictions, tell him about them. This may well have a great effect on how he handles your case. It is better he should learn of

your "priors" before going to court than have the D.A. spring them on him after he has built his defense around the belief that you are a first-time offender.

6. There is no need for you to dress like a skid-row derelict when visiting your lawyer for the first time. Dress modestly and conservatively, however. A display of expensive clothing and jewelry spells *money* to the lawyer. You dressed to impress him. You *did* impress him. He'll up his fee accordingly.

b) Felonies—"The Fear Game"

Section 23101 of the California Vehicle Code reads: "Felony drunk driving:

"Any person who, while under the influence of intoxicating liquor or under the combined influence of intoxicating liquor and any drug, drives a vehicle and when so driving does any act forbidden by law or neglects any duty imposed by law in the driving of such vehicle, which act or neglect proximately causes bodily injury to any person other than himself is *guilty of a felony* and upon conviction thereof shall be punished by *imprisonment in the state prison* for not less than one year nor more than *five years* or in the county jail for not less than 90 days nor more than one year *and* by a fine of not less than $250.00 nor more than *$5,000*." (The italics are mine)

Frighten you? It certainly frightens many first-timers who, when the words I have emphasized above are emphasized to them by an attorney reading the statute aloud, realize they could go to prison for five years and pay a $5,000 fine as well. The seed of the fear game is sown. The unethical lawyer will see that it grows until it bears fruit.

What the shyster will fail to tell the first-timer is that the chances of a heavy fine or of a prison term are usually quite remote. Very early in my career I recall handling a case arising under this 23101 statute. The client could have been a double for Grandma Moses. White-haired, kindly and shy, this seventy-five-year-old lady had proceeded to get very drunk one evening. While driving home without headlights on, she had hit a man who was changing the tire of his car well off the roadway. My client passed out. The man suffered a permanently crippled left leg. Witnesses were available. Grandma failed a variety of drunk driving tests given to her by the police. There was no doubt she was guilty and such a plea was entered with the court. My plan was to work on the probation officer to whom the case had been assigned for the sentencing recommendation. We stressed her age, and the fact that this was her first offense and that, aside from this lapse, she was a perfectly swell, all-around citizen. The pay-off was an excellent report from the P.O. He recommended no jail time and a small fine payable in installments. Judges follow probation reports nine times out of ten but our judge hit the proverbial roof. He was outraged. His sentence was that she spend six months in the county jail (this was later commuted to three months because of good behavior). Considering the wording of the statute, however, this was not such a bad result.

The fear game is not played by predicting the ultimate result of the case. Stressed, instead, is the possible prison term and heavy fine. The lawyer talks about "possible" but he does it in such a way that the client is thinking "probable." Visualizing himself sent away for five years, the client is scared right out of his wallet. The fine alone might wipe him out. His lawyer offers hope. *He* can get the client out of this mess with a minimum of jail time* or a much smaller fine than outlined in the statute. But for all the work that requires to be done he must be adequately com-

---

*In the case of the 75-year-old Grandma Moses type, the client would probably not have gone to jail had her victim not been crippled for life. This is what infuriated the judge.

pensated—better a big fee than a bigger fine; better the fee than prison time. The lawyer is so sure he can do well that the client agrees to the fee, paying in cash or hocking the family home, car or jewels. In the end the outcome is as the lawyer predicted. The client leaves, singing his praises. Little does the client know that Joe Doakes, just out of law school and charging far lower fees (because he hasn't learned the games yet) could have achieved the same results.

Another money-making idea that will be coming back into vogue as more and more lawyers inundate the community is the old "I need extra money to pay off the judge and/or D.A." A popular game in Tammany Hall days and even as late as the 1930s, it once even had some truth in it. Some judges and D.A.'s could be paid off. Today, the average judge is a better and more ethical man than were his predecessors. Prosecutors, better paid and more secure than in earlier years, are not about to give up what they have for penny ante bribes. Even so, I heard several years ago of an attorney who successfully pulled this trick (the person telling me would not divulge his name). He was, of course, playing on his client's fear. The scenario went like this:

Attorney: "I'll also need an extra $1,000 to get the right judge and pay him off."

Client: "You can do that?"

Attorney: "You bet I can. Remember, you could go to prison for this one."

The client took the bait and forked over the $1,000.

The hearing day arrived. The client, sitting in the courtroom, saw his lawyer whispering to the clerk. Moments later he was admitted to the judge's chambers. The "personal matter" the lawyer wanted to chat with the judge about was a game of golf that coming Friday, or perhaps some recent court ruling, but nothing was mentioned about bribes. Five or ten minutes later the client saw his mouthpiece re-entering the courtroom. The lawyer winked at the client and gave the old V-for-victory sign. Even if the D.A. had gone into chambers with him he would have had a story for the client—that he had to split the $1,000 between the judge and the D.A. The case ended as the lawyer promised it would, just as had a similar case the week before. Young Joe Doakes could have achieved the same result without so much as seeing the judge since the judge's ruling was simply normal court policy in a case of this type. Smart lawyer, happy but ignorant client.

Fear is an emotion that often causes us to take leave of our senses. The unethical lawyer, knowing this, stresses the "heavy" portions of the law which the client is alleged to have violated. He can make promises to the client that he knows can't be kept so as to secure a bigger fee. Later, when the court's decision is contrary to his prediction, he can blame it on the trial judge ("The presiding judge sent us to a bad courtroom") or the jury ("This jury panel is the worst I've ever seen"). If the client complains to the bar association it will be his word against the lawyer's as to what was promised. Chances are he won't complain. Very few do, and lawyers know it.

* * *

What you can do about the fear game

1. The suggestions listed after "Misdemeanor games" can be applied in felony cases as well. Use them all.

2. In felony matters try not to let fear either show in your face or disturb your normal thinking processes. Naturally, felonies inspire more fear than do their little brothers, the misdemeanors; but if the fee-hunting attorney notes your fear, and sees that it's troubling you mightily, he will go to work on it in order to justify a larger fee. Stay cool. Inquire at length into the policy of local courts for a first- or second-timer being hit by the charges that confront you in court. Should the attorney indicate that the maximum penalty, both as to

fine and imprisonment, is the local policy then he is probably kidding you. Rarely does this happen. I have seen people with a "prior sheet" a page long, walk away with six month jail terms and probation terms that, though rather stringent, nevertheless allow them to walk the streets again. Many repeaters go out and "do it again" because they know their penalties will be light. There just aren't enough jails or prisons for it to be possible to send every offender away for the maximum term prescribed by law. The repeater, knowing this, keeps coming back to court. Some day he may commit one crime too many but he always figures he's good for just one more. First and second offenders, then, should not be too frightened about the outcome of their cases; nor should they let their attorneys frighten them.

c) The "Cash fee" Game

It will make no difference to you, generally speaking, whether you pay a fee by cash or check to your attorney. Should you end up in the hands of a ne'er-do-well lawyer, however, it could make a difference, directly or indirectly, and so should be discussed.

Through the trial stage, criminal cases are bang-bang operations (appeals may go on for years). The time between arrest and conviction is relatively short in comparison with the start-to-finish times involved in civil and probate matters. The fee you pay a criminal lawyer at the start of proceedings is generally "it." There is an age-old saying in criminal law work: "Get your fee in advance because, win or lose, you'll never get it afterwards." The trained criminal law attorney will follow this adage. If he fails to get the fee he will not take the case.

In criminal law cases fees are paid in cash far more than in any other type of case. This fact may be attributed to:

(i) Persons of very modest means rarely seem to have checking accounts. They exchange their weekly wages for money orders to pay their regular bills. Other expenditures (including payment of attorney fees) are generally paid in cash;

(ii) The attorney requesting a cash fee;

(iii) The attorney requesting part of the fee be paid in cash (when a check is tendered) so that this cash may be "spread around the courthouse" to insure a good result;

(iv) The client not trusting banks (there are still a lot of those folks around) and therefore having no checking account.

Many people to whom I have talked over the years have stated that in criminal law cases in which they were defendants, their attorneys never gave them receipts for their cash payment. One said he asked for a receipt but was told by the attorney that there was no point in having one since the fee wasn't tax deductible; the client insisted, however, and got his receipt. Another asked for a receipt but, having just shelled out $1,000 in cash, saw the receipt for only $750. The attorney's bland reply to his obvious query was that he had to spread some money around and naturally this couldn't be listed as personal income. Try the game yourself if you are so unfortunate as to be charged with a crime. Once the attorney names a fee give it to him in cash. See if he gives you a receipt without your asking for one; if he does he's ethical. Try a check and see if he asks, instead, for cash; if he does he's probably in the unethical or at least borderline shady-practice category.

Why cash? Well, criminal cases are quick, one-shot deals. Rarely do defendants appeal their felony convictions, and still more rarely their misdemeanor convictions. The file may be opened and closed in a month. After it is closed the file can be destroyed and often is. How, then, can the I.R.S., on an audit, determine the cases this lawyer had or what his fees were? Disposable appointment books also make it impossible to see who visited the lawyer. Many case files will be kept, of course, and many appointments will still be reflected on the secretary's calendar. A person can't live in apparent wealth as a lawyer when he has *no* files and his calendars reflect *no* appointments! The I.R.S. sees the top of the iceberg. They may guess that much lies unseen below the surface, but the cost of proving it is so immense that the taxmen rarely dive after it unless they feel a whole lot of money is involved. Those who don't report cash incomes (and lawyers are not the only people who don't) soon learn to buy material things only with their reported incomes; homes, yachts, cars and country club memberships fall into this category. The unreported cash is spent on the races, on liquor, on brief trips under assumed names, and on other consumable items that can't be traced.

Most criminal law attorneys apparently report their entire incomes. Yet the temptation not to report is so great in this cash income field that the percentage of lawyers not reporting income in criminal case work is probably higher than in other legal fields. If ten lawyers practicing criminal law each earn $100,000 in a given year and if these ten, on average, report only seventy-five percent of their incomes, then $250,000 is going unreported. But ten is a ridiculous figure. Considering that there are over 450,000 lawyers in our country, it can be said without hesitation that at least 5,000 of these may be hiding an average of twenty-five percent of their fees. These 5,000, at $100,000 per, earn five hundred million dollars. Reporting only seventy-five percent of it leaves *$125,000,000* unreported, tax-free dollars. There is no doubt in my mind, after twenty-eight years of listening and observing, that this figure is probably still too low. What does all this mean to you?

First of all we know that the government, be it local, state or federal, runs on *your* tax money. We know the government likes to spend money and each year finds new ways to spend even more money. If not enough money is coming in then taxes are raised. Unreported dollars, if found, can be taxed. If enough are found then perhaps—just perhaps—taxes won't be raised or, if raised, not so high as might have been expected. You, as a taxpayer, will reap the benefits. How to aid in getting more of this unreported money into the taxation picture will be outlined below in defenses against the criminal law cash game.

Secondly, if you ever wish to complain to the bar association about something you allege your attorney did wrong in a criminal lawsuit, it may come down to how much you paid him. Without a receipt it's your word against his. Naturally, he may claim the amount was smaller than it actually was out of fear that you may inform the I.R.S. of the payment. A "your word against mine" situation is a stalemate which nobody wins. Get a receipt in any case, criminal or otherwise, and keep it!

What you can do about the cash fee game

1. Always get a receipt for your payment(s) whether by cash, check or otherwise.

2. Don't fall for the "cash under the table" routine—money supposedly to be spread around to help your case. It's a phony. Get up, get out and get another lawyer.

3. Check your receipt before leaving the office, making sure the amount shown on the receipt is the amount you paid.

4. If the attorney insists on cash, stick by your guns if you prefer to write a check. Should you eventually pay cash, ask him

(a) to write you a receipt, and

(b) why he prefers cash.

Lawyer: "It takes time for checks to clear and I must get started right away."

Client: "Local checks clear overnight and you could call my bank now to verify that it's good."

5. Secure an attorney recommended by the local bar association or by a friend who used him with good results. This attorney, knowing of the referral, will be less likely to play the "cash game."

CHAPTER 5

Ambulance Chasing

The tinkle of cocktail glasses, the chatter of voices. A late afternoon party is underway on the patio of a suburban home. Here and there the sounds of laughter, now and then the breaking of a slippery glass.

Suddenly the two lawyers who are present stop in mid-talk. They are intent on listening. Each has heard the wail of a faraway siren. No one else in the entire party has noticed it.

Is it the siren of a police car, a fire truck or, hopefully, an ambulance? The trained ears of the lawyers seek the answer. The party is now a million miles away. The people talking to them are in another world.

One of the lawyers dashes toward the door. The siren, drawing nearer, is that of an ambulance. The other attorney, not quite sure yet, but noticing his colleague racing away, quickly follows suit. By the time he reaches his car the first attorney is already driving away, tires screeching. The ambulance hoves into view a block away, rushing through an intersection. The first lawyer gives chase.

Lawyer Number Two is cursing. His car picks this moment not to start. He watches first the ambulance, then the other lawyer, disappear from his view.

"Damn it!" he finally says, giving up and sliding out of the car. "I only hope it wasn't an accident that damned ambulance was going to!"

If it was an accident, lawyer number one will be there, business card in hand, to aid the victims. Those victims who, in his quickly-formed judgment, appear to have been in the right in the accident will get the bulk of his attention.

Lawyer number two is back at martini time again, cursing his luck. *C'est la vie!* There'll be another day.

* * *

Maude Imahurtin is watching TV in her small apartment. Her two broken legs, heavily-encased in plaster, are propped up on a small stool in front of her chair. Whatever Mary Hartman goes through tonight will be nothing compared to what Maude has undergone this past week in the hospital. "Medical Center" seems so tame this evening that she switches to another program.

There's a knock on her door, then another. Who could it be at this time of night?

"Who's there?"

"You Maude Imahurtin who was involved in the auto accident a week ago at 12th and Cherry?"

"Y-yes," Maude answers, thinking it must finally be someone from the other driver's insurance company.

"I'm investigating the matter and would like to speak with you for a few minutes," says the calm and pleasant voice on the other side of the door.

Maude wearily picks up her two crutches, staggers up and painfully makes her way to the door.

" 'Bout time someone came," she mutters as she slips the four dead bolts and opens the door.

A pleasant-looking young man, armed with a briefcase and holding a business card toward her, steps across the threshold. Unnoticed by her, his eyes beam when he sees her plaster-encased legs.

She begins to ask him to come in but by then he is already seating himself on the davenport and opening his briefcase. She glances at his card.

ISLEGO & GETTUM
Private Investigators
2933 Prarie St.,
Yourtown, U.S.A.

"You are Mr.——?"

"Gettum. Jim Gettum, ma'am," he responds.

"Courteous young fellow," she thinks, "and so handsome."

"I'm here about your accident."

"Yes. I guessed you were."

Jim gets down to brass tacks. He has a copy of the police report (this should indicate he's "on" the case). For the next ten minutes Maude rarely gets to say anything save "Yes, sir" or "No, sir" as Gettum questions her concerning the accident and her injuries. He goes into great detail about her injuries, who her doctors were, what was done for her in the hospital, when she is to see the doctor again—so many questions her head is beginning to ache. As if noting her pained expression, Gettum pauses.

"You from the insurance company?" Maude finally gets to ask.

"No, ma'am. Better than that. I'm the investigator for Hugo Chasem, the famous attorney."

"Never heard of him."

"Probably your first accident."

"It was."

"Then it may be natural you've never heard of Mr. Chasem. He deals exclusively with auto accident cases. Those who have had him, sing his praises. You don't read about him in the papers because he is more concerned with making money for his clients than he is with publicity. He got a settlement of $250,000 for a client last year. Here, I'll show you a copy of the settlement check." (Shows her the copy, quickly puts it back in his briefcase.)

"What's that got to do with me?"

"He heard about your accident. It really made him mad—the other car striking yours the way it did and the driver being drunk as he was. He hates drunk drivers. Being the sole support of his aged mother, he also has a special compassion for older people. He sent me out there as soon as he heard you were out of the hospital, to see if he could do anything for you."

"What could *he* do for me?" Maude naively

answers, smelling no rats, seeing only the kindly man across the room from her.

Gettum goes on to explain that Mr. Chasem would like to handle her case. He would bear all the court costs—filing fees, depositions if needed and investigative expenses. When she recovered a settlement, and there was no doubt she would, these moneys could be repaid to Mr. Chasem, then and only then. If by some odd quirk of fate he recovered nothing for her she owed him nothing, not even reimbursement for the moneys he'd spent. He would be out of pocket all that money, and just because he liked her and her case that much.

"I—— suppose he'll charge a fee for all this," Maude says cautiously.

Her guest quickly agrees that his employer can't handle these cases for nothing. But, he goes on to explain, he takes them on a contingent fee basis.

"That is," he hurriedly continues, seeing question marks written all over her face when he hits the word "contingent," "he will take a percentage of what you recover. Again, if you recover nothing—supposing the insurance company goes broke or something like that—you owe him *nothing*. It's like, really, his handling the case for nothing. You put up no money, but in the end you recover money."

"How much is this, what did you call it, contingent fee he'll charge?" Maude asks, only inches now from being convinced.

By now Gettum, an old hand at this game, has sized her up. A shrewd analyst, he figures Maude as one who would turn down a high fee (fifty percent) but would go the low to medium "jump route."

"Just 25 percent of anything he settles for before filing suit, one third after suit is filed, and [pausing] 35 percent if we go to trial." He was going to say 40 percent [as he usually did] but her case was a good one and probably would be settled well before trial time. No point in scaring her off.

"That sounds reasonable," Maude says slowly, still not absolutely sure.

"*More* than reasonable, Mrs. Imahurtin . . ."

"*Miss* Imahurtin. I'm a maiden lady."

"Sorry. As I was saying, more than reasonable. Most lawyers *start* at one third and go up to fifty percent. Most lawyers make *you* pay the court costs and investigation costs. These sometimes run into a lot of dollars."

"Well, Mr. Gettum, he certainly sounds like the man for me."

"He is, he is. He does all the work and you just stay here and get well. There's a bonus too! If you run short of money because of doctor bills, he'll advance you money from time to time, so sure is he that this case will be settled."

"What a nice man this Mr. Chasem must be."

"They don't come any better."

Quietly and smoothly he draws out the Chasem/client attorney fee contract. Maude signs.

He gives her authorization forms to sign, papers allowing her doctors and hospital to release information to him. She signs, smiling with happiness she hasn't known since that drunk slammed into her car.

Gettum packs away the papers, bids a fond adieu and leaves. Hugo Chasem, attorney-at-law, has just secured another case.

* * *

The two stories you have just read are tales of ambulance chasing. The public is inclined to believe the cocktail party gambit. Isn't that just like a lawyer!

They are not inclined to believe Maude's story. It would take too much gall to pull a stunt like that, going out and signing up a case without even calling in advance. Who would have the nerve?

Chasem would have the nerve, and the gall, to put someone up to a stunt like that. In Gettum he finds a blood brother, a man who perhaps has more gall and nerve than he has himself. Chasem, after all, just stays in the background.

The signing stunt that Gettum pulled off is done on a regular basis across the face of the nation. Even as you read this, someone, somewhere, is signing a contract allowing an "ambulance chasing" lawyer to handle his or her case. Many thousands do it yearly. Rarely, these days, will you find an attorney at the scene of an accident handing out cards; that's passe. Today's style consists of letting a friend or investigator (usually the latter) do your dirty work for you. Only in desperation will the attorney himself go out to solicit business from a potential client who did not request his visit.

Legal ethics require that the client contact the attorney for an appointment, not vice versa. The contact made vice versa is, pure and simple, "ambulance chasing" and is the bane of every bar association in the land. Not a week passes but legal newspapers (and more and more often regular daily newspapers) are printing news stories of crackdowns on lawyers for ambulance chasing. The trouble is, though, that for every ten who do it, maybe only one gets caught.

In the days before bar associations, or when similar associations were too weak to do anything about it, many a lawyer procured business through the chasing of ambulances. As the victim lay bloody and semiconscious, the shyster would sign him up to the ever-ready contract of attorney-employment. The definition "ambulance chaser" carried over into other fields. Hardly had rigor mortis completed its tour of a rich man's body when his widow would be visited by lawyers seeking the probate of the estate. Criminals would be pursued by lawyers seeking their cases— though this still happens. For example, dozens of Los Angeles attorneys visited Charles Manson in his jail cell while he was awaiting trial. He had asked very few of them to visit him. Most saw him on their own, seeking to try his case. They were not after money for he had none, but they were chasing the rainbow of publicity that would arch over this long and exciting trial. Everything changes, but nothing really changes. Ambulances are still being chased.

As lawyers must sometimes be in court and cannot be everywhere at once, it became their practice to employ runners or "cappers" to secure business for them. Investigator Jim Gettum, who visited Maude Imahurtin, was a "runner." In the old days in England, such men were actually referred to as runners. Modern sophistication has taught them to "run" under the title of private investigator.

The word "capper," a term often applied to lawyers' runners, has much the same connotation as the old English term "puffer." These persons, without having any intention to purchase, were employed by auctioneers to raise prices by constantly bidding upwards, knowing all the while they were not bound by their bids. The name "capper," or "decoy duck" or "by bidder", was also given to such a person because he capped the bidding for the auctioneer; when he had bid high enough the auctioneer would give him a secret code signal not to bid again against the last legitimate bid. The sale was then "capped" by the auctioneer accepting this last bid. It was easy to transfer the word "capper" to a lawyer's runner because he, of course, capped cases for his attorney employer. With the contract signed, no other lawyer could take the case. The bidding had ended.

"Barratry" is a term often used to denote the practice of ambulance chasing. According to Ballentine's Law Dictionary, the word is defined as: "Habitually stirring up quarrels and (law) suits." Webster defines it better by calling it the "persistent incitement of litigation," viz., stirring up trouble that leads to the filing of lawsuits.

So what's wrong with a lawyer going out and finding business on his own? Salesmen do it all the time and, after all, a lawyer is but a salesman. Melvin Belli, the gregarious, personable winner of cases, sells himself to juries during trials and to the general public via TV and books.

Selling is satisfactory so long as the attorney stays within the confines of ethics. He can write books, appear on TV, run for office and give speeches, all of these being activities which "advertise" the fact that he's a lawyer.

But cappers, runners and ambulance chasers? *Verboten!* The reason they are condemned by legal ethics is that the law has always considered that it is members of the general public who should visit lawyers, not the other way round. Maude Imahurtin might well have settled her case with the insurance company or, later, had she needed a lawyer, she might have been referred to one by a friend or by the local bar association. By signing her up, Chasem, through Gettum, was inciting litigation, adding a case to the already overburdened court calendar. He was making a case out of something that might not have been a case. Through suavity, personality and, probably, a superior and more experienced mind, Gettum was able to force his will on Maude. In effect he was holding her hand as she signed the contract. She thought she was doing it of her own free will but it was really Gettum's will, not hers, that was in operation. Chasem, the attorney who had selected Gettum, was the chief offender because he had paid Gettum to do just what he did and had worked out the sign-up system with him.

The better lawyers don't chase ambulances or employ runners, nor do they encourage friends to incite litigation. They are content to live on their reputations, securing business either through satisfied clients referring others, or by engaging in public "advertising" condoned by the bar—speeches, political ads, books, TV appearances, club work, church work and volunteering their services at P.T.A. meetings.

People who sign up with runners or with attorneys who drop by without invitation are, in the main, signing up with shyster lawyers. They are bad news to their clients for their interest is more in making money for themselves than in looking for the very best results for their clients. With the alarming annual increase in the number of lawyers, is likely to come a proportional increase in the practice of ambulance chasing. Not only the *true* shyster (the lawyer who is a bad guy 100 percent of the time) but also some lawyers who are hard up for business will seek litigation through this means. Pure of heart and mind as most lawyers are when they leave law school, many of them will bend the rules a bit to stay out of the bread lines. Capping is one way of doing it. Older lawyers, stifled by the competition now that everybody and his brother want to become lawyers, may also get in the chase. The better lawyers will continue to prosper, however, in their customary ethical fashion.

In addition to the risk of signing up with a shyster, the capper's victim runs the risk of signing up with an attorney who is inexperienced, incompetent or for some reason hard up (and who, in this last case, will settle cheaply so as to make a quick buck). He may find himself getting less money out of a good lawsuit than he would have if his lawyer had been both ethical and competent. Furthermore, his suit may end disastrously—if his lawyer either abandons the case after taking the retainer (this sin is on the increase) or, being inexpert, louses things up at the trial and loses.

A good example of what can happen to the client in this kind of situation recently arose in a conversation I had with an insurance adjuster. He told me of a visit he'd recently made to a small but busy downtown Los Angeles law firm. So tremendous was their volume of business that every month of the year he visited them to settle cases; since he represented only one of dozens of liability insurance carriers in the area it could be supposed that many other adjusters saw this firm every day of the month. They were known as "settlers" (viz., lawyers who would rather settle cases than have them tried) and it was reputed that they did considerable ambulance chasing. One of the partners had bragged of their office always having several thousand personal injury cases going at one time. From what my adjuster friend could see, they were being truthful in this numbers claim. A small office just doesn't have that many cases without a feeder system of "runners"—investigators, ambulance drivers, hospital attendants and, occasionally perhaps, the un-ethical doctor.

A case the adjuster had recently seen them about appeared to have a settlement value of around $3,000. Face to face with the lawyer this sum was agreed upon. Then, snapping his fingers as though in afterthought, the lawyer opined that maybe he'd best check the file one more time to make sure; it had been several months since he'd looked at it. The secretary found it after some search (it should have been on the lawyer's desk during the adjuster's visit). Lo and be-hold, the lawyer found in scanning the file that the client had had a relapse and the medical bills alone were now well over the $3,000 mark. This being a good case of liability, the lawyer thought he'd better hold off settling for awhile. Wise decision, but the lawyer seemed a bit hurt that he couldn't, even in bad con-science, make a quick dollar that day. The attorney could have settled on the spot, the adjuster advised me, because he had blanket written authority from his client to sign drafts *and* releases. *Never give your at-torney, even a good, ethical-to-the-core one, such authority!*

The adjuster went on to say that he had settled many a case with that firm at less than he, the adjuster, felt the attorneys could have secured had they held out a bit longer and/or gone to trial. It is at trial time, or even when the jury is out, that carriers come up with their final final, top top dollar offers. He had heard, from other adjusters, that they had had the same ex-periences with this firm. The name of the firm? He wouldn't tell me. How did he know I wouldn't blow the whistle on them? Insurance carriers wanted the firm to stay in business. After all, they were saving many thousands of dollars annually in settling with these quick-buck artists.

There is no week in the year that newspapers in the

Library

Main

1301 Olive

241-2288

~~~~~~

Apt. 721-1229

Rent mo. $

rm.

6600

Clayton + Kraft

N/E Side

East of Skinner

Coffee

~~Bleach~~ / Powder

diapers

~~Banana~~ / Apple

~~Grapefruit~~ / kettle

~~Cotton balls~~ —

98	37
98	37
98	14
196	37
	11

Los Angeles area don't carry some story about the state bar cracking down on ambulance chasers. The chasers' modus operandi is generally the same as in Maude's case—the investigator or well-meaning friend scours the bushes for cases. Last year a number of people connected with a local hospital were discharged for feeding cases to selected attorneys. Not a few ambulance drivers have lost their jobs because they gave immediate news of accident victims to lawyers who paid them for the information.

In years past the runner, capper and ambulance attendant escaped legal punishment for this activity on behalf of the lawyer boss. While the boss was disbarred or suspended for long periods, the investigator and friends went about their business as usual. Hospital personnel might lose their jobs but they could always find work elsewhere. A movement is now afoot, however, to impose criminal sanctions, fines and/or jail time, on those found to be soliciting business for lawyers on a mass scale. These are not your satisfied clients referring friends, but people hired by the attorney to scout up business for him on a regular basis. Once such legislation comes into being, a runner will think twice or thrice about getting involved and we will find fewer of his ilk in the field of law practice. Why, for a few bucks, should he stick his neck out when the attorney for whom he works is the guy making the real money?

In my own experience over the years, I have lost several cases to capping attorneys. In each instance, I asked the almost-client to back me up in a complaint to the state bar, because the lawyer signing him up had committed an illegal act, but all refused me. None of them wanted to get involved.

"If you get me mixed up in this I'll tell the bar that I picked the lawyer out myself," one of them retorted.

Two other cases that I can recall losing to capping lawyers ended in the same manner. My lost clients were so overwhelmed by their new attorneys that they took great umbrage at my suggestion that we turn

them in to the state bar. Without the client to back up
the charge, nothing will come of it.

My first such loss to an ambulance-chasing attorney
came as a great shock. As a young lawyer is shocked
the first time he finds a client has been lying to him, so
is he shocked the first time a fellow attorney steals a
case from him.

My first such experience was typical of all of them.
The client called late one afternoon for an appoint-
ment. We set it up for eleven the following morning.
Had I known what was going to transpire that evening
I'd have rushed out to see him as soon as I'd hung up
the phone!

By noon the next day the client hadn't shown or
called. I rang him up. Was there any problem?

"Yes," he said, "I've already got another lawyer."

To a lawyer, the loss of a case is like the loss of a
paycheck. How, why, had I lost this one?

"Well, when I was home last night, someone
knocked on the door. Turned out to be a lawyer [the
almost-client gave me his name] and his investigator.
Showed me his credentials, very impressive. Specializes in my kind of case. Said you were a nice guy but
too young to have had any experience, best I sign with
him. So I did."

I was flabbergasted.

If I complained to the state bar, would my almost-
client back me up? No way! Even though the lawyer
had come to his home, he had picked him out. If I
caused any trouble he would tell the bar that he had
called the lawyer. That would show me, wouldn't it?

Sure would!

I took the matter up with an older member of the
local bar association. After being told all the facts, including the lost client's refusal to help me, he advised
me to forget about it. It would be my word against the
older lawyer's. The latter, with *his* client to back him
up, and with some stature in the bar, would win. I
would leave the hearing with egg on my face and the
word would soon spread around town that I was a

troublemaker. He advised me to forget about it, and let it drop.

One time our bar association undertook an investigation of a certain lawyer who, it appeared, was being fed a steady diet of criminal cases by someone working in the local jailhouse. I remember the occasion well because our bar association blew $1,200 (its total budget for outside activities) on investigators. "Blew" is the word because nothing came of it. Evidence was found at every turn but all of it combined did not add up to the proof that any prosecutor requires to convict. What you know in your heart and what you can *prove* in court are often two different animals.

When the investigation was completed no less than five local attorneys had turned up in the investigator's net as being recipients of criminal cases from jailers, the police, or bail bondsmen. As local bar associations have no power to punish, the entire matter was then tied in a ribbon and presented to the state bar. Nothing ever came of it. That was many years ago when the state bar was less active in prosecuting offenders of the legal ethics code. Today, there would probably be a different ending to the story.

Lawyers, even ones of good repute, are far more prone to cut each other's throats than the members of any other of the professions. Probates, divorces and many other cases are stolen away each year from one lawyer by another. The theft takes place when the thieving attorney opines that, "while your lawyer is a good enough guy, I'm far better in that particular field of law than he is. Maybe you'd better switch to me." More often than one would believe, the client does so. This activity can best be described as "after capping." It is the soliciting of a case that another attorney already has, a case that may even be well underway in the courts. Prosecution is difficult because the key witness, the client, will stick by her/his new attorney and there goes the proof of the stealing. This fact of life is known to every attorney save the very young one, and he generally finds out sooner rather than later.

Before considering what you, the public, can do to curtail ambulance chasing, consider some of the events in your own life. What, for example, would you think of a "friend" who was constantly running down others, many of whom you liked? What would you do if, given a gift, you were told it had been stolen? What of a person who entered your home under false pretenses and then proceeded to try to sell you books, or a vacuum cleaner? If a person spends much of his time telling you how wonderful he is, would you not suspect that he was covering up his own insecurity or his own *lack* of abilities? Action always speaks louder than words. Have you always considered legal matters as goods of trade that are to be hustled and sold at bargain and below, in the manner of a merchant's sidewalk sale? Is your once-in-a-lifetime case such a cheap bit of merchandise that you would sell it to the lowest bidder or give it to the first lawyer who came along and asked for it? If your replies are in the negative then perhaps you can aid the legal profession in cleansing its ranks of one of its more scurrilous offenders—the capping, puffing, running ambulance chaser and his entourage of paid stooges.

What you can do about ambulance chasing

1. You have a case against somebody. An investigator knocks on your door and advises that he is there concerning your lawsuit. Determine immediately whether or not he is representing the opposing party. Should he advise you he is, then, once inside, advise to the contrary, kick him out. If he is seeking to represent you in your legal matter don't let him come inside in the first place. Such persons, no matter how handsome, polite, friendly and charming, are runners. They represent shysters, and shysters you can do without. A bonus from such a visit will be your newfound

knowledge that someone thinks you have a good case. Someone has taken the trouble to come by your home to sign you up. Best now that you call a friend, or the bar association, to secure the name(s) of a competent attorney specializing in the field relevant to your case.

2. If you are satisfied with the lawyer you have, keep him. Should another lawyer, whether met at a party or anywhere else, give your lawyer the knock and try to get you to switch to him, turn a deaf ear to his entreaties. Who wants a braggart and a name-caller for a lawyer? What sort of a lawyer is he who must get business by running down others?

In California, it is said (and from what I have seen, I believe it) that in contested divorce matters the wife/client will change lawyers at least once prior to trial and often three or more times. If, for some good reason, you should want to switch lawyers, then your best recommendation for a new one will come, as these pages have stressed so often, through a friend *who has had the lawyer and was satisfied with him* or through the local bar association. Even then, should your new lawyer spend much of his time "knocking" your former lawyer while bragging of his own prowess in a particular field of law, you should perhaps look elsewhere for an attorney. The new attorney, if he's good, may see the former attorney's errors, if any (many times only a lawyer/client personality clash has caused the client to go lawyer-seeking again), but he will not spend time talking of these or bragging about how well he will do for you. He will quietly go about correcting the errors and, instead of talking, *work*. In court the well-prepared lawyer, not the blustering, orating, half-prepared lawyer, will win the day.

3. Should ambulance drivers or hospital attendants slip you the business card of a lawyer, report those persons to their employers. Each will undoubtedly have an excuse for having given you the card ("Gee, I was just trying to help the fellow out!"), and it may be the excuse is valid. Nevertheless, if that person is a paid runner for a lawyer, he/she will think twice about

giving out business cards again. To be caught a second time might mean loss of job. Is it worth it? Never!

If a jailer gives you the name of a "damned good criminal attorney," thank him, but, when free or when able to use the phone, call someone else. A lawyer with a pipeline to a jail will usually have more business than he can handle and your case may well be lost in the shuffle. You want a lawyer who will devote his time to your case for the purpose of securing the best result for you.

Policemen and bail bondsmen sometimes *do* give people the names of lawyers as favors, though usually they do not get paid for it. About the only way of telling who these lawyers are is when the policeman or bail bondsman is a little too insistent that you see one particular lawyer or may "just happen" to have that lawyer's card on him.

"Do you have one of his business cards?" you might inquire.

"Sure," the errant police officer or bondsman will reply, pulling out a stack of his friend's cards and peeling one off for you.

This is your tip-off. The guy is probably capping—get another lawyer.

4. Tell your friends, neighbors and near relatives to be wary of any lawyer soliciting their business, whether directly or through a runner. These lawyers are unethical. Judges in your area probably know it too and, facing a judge at trial's end with an unethical lawyer at your side, you may find some of the tarnish rubbing off on you, or your friends and relatives. See your local bar association for the better lawyers, and follow the association's recommendations.

CHAPTER 6

Embezzlement

a) The nature of the beast

Ballentine's Law Dictionary defines embezzlement as the "fraudulent conversion of another's personal property by one to whom it has been entrusted (sic), with the intention of depriving the owner thereof."

The crime of embezzlement will vary from state to state because it is a creature of statute (written law). It was unknown in the old days of common law (unwritten law). In that bygone era, to take money entrusted to your keeping by another and then use it for your own purposes was a type of theft—petty or grand, depending on the amount involved. It was sometimes called "robbery" if done under forceful circumstances. When common law slowly disappeared into the written laws of the various states, the crime of thieving from the moneys of another, or the taking of his property, all of which you were holding for him in trust, came to be called "embezzlement."

The old Century Dictionary carried one of the earliest definitions of the term "embezzle." There it was said that to embezzle was to misappropriate or misspend both

(a) on a permanent basis, and

(b) even when the taker intended to restore the money or property in due time.

Then, as now, the crux of the crime was that the money or properties taken had, initially, been given to the wrongdoer by another to hold in trust for him. The crime was the breach of this trust as opposed, for example, to burglarizing a home, robbing a bank or stealing a stranger's auto.

The difficulty with the embezzlement game is that no one can ever determine whether the embezzler intended to keep the money/property permanently or to return it later. Every person caught at the game will swear on a stack of Bibles that he intended to return the money. But it makes no difference, really, because the definition covers both permanent and temporary takings.

Just as there are little white lies, so there are also little white embezzlements. All of us have been guilty of these. Your son gave you $5 to hold for him. While he was at school one day the Fuller Brush man came by with your order, and the bill came to $5. You didn't have that much in your purse or billfold, so guess how the Fuller Brush man was paid? Of course you intended to repay your son the $5 and did so. But a "little white embezzlement" had occurred. Easy to do? You bet!

The crime of conversion is a blood brother of embezzlement. This usually concerns taking another's property, converting it to your own use—and being caught while using it. Even though the property had been entrusted to you, you might be charged with conversion rather than embezzlement. You might, as an example, be given use of a car to drive to the drugstore a mile away but be found, hours later, riding around at the beach. You've committed a crime.

The temptation to embezzle probably lies dormant within all of us. The mechanics of your borrowing your son's $5 to pay off the Fuller Brush man are the same mechanics that the criminally-charged embezzler employs. You were borrowing with the intent to repay; so was he. Beyond the range of "borrowing" small sums at home, however, the average person will never be tempted by sums large enough to convert him into a criminally charged embezzler. Most of us will vow to the Almighty that we could resist the temptation, but how do we know, never having been *really* tempted? The largest sum I've ever held for another was $50,000. I held it for a week and hadn't the slightest temptation to touch it. This was not a true test, however, because

(a) I wasn't starving at the time, and

(b) at the end of the week the client would pay me $15,000 of that sum as a fee. On the other hand, what would the situation have been had I been a race-track devotee or a confirmed high-stakes poker player? Do I have a price? Do you?

Question: A friend gives you one million dollars to hold for him for a year. He will be in Timbuktu and completely out of communication with you during that time. Would you, during that year, use any of this one million dollars for your own purposes if you felt you really *needed* something?

Answer: "Well, probably, but I'd pay it back before the year was over!"

Question: "What if your son gave you one dollar to hold for him for a day. Would you spend that if need arose?"

Answer: "Of course not, what do you think I am?!"

Question: "We've established what you are. I'm just trying to find out the degree."

The gist of embezzlement is simply a breach of the trust reposed in someone by another, the breach being the taking of money or property so entrusted. When you deposit money in a bank you are trusting that bank to give you back your money on demand. Legion are the people from the Depression years of the thirties who could tell you how their bankers skipped town with *their* money and the bank folded. Not a month goes by but some newspaper, somewhere, reports the story of a trusted bank employee "going south" with X number of dollars. Of all of us, bankers and stock-brokers have the greatest opportunity to embezzle on a continuing basis. Yet they are so tied up with rules, regulations, accountings and the ever-watchful eye of the boss, that the embezzlements in these fields are probably far fewer, percentagewise, than even a decade ago and previously.

Just how many embezzlements occur in our country

each year will never be known. Most end up being "safe embezzlements"—the money or property is replaced before the other party finds out it's been taken at all.

"Whew! That was a close one. Got the money back before Aunt Harriet knew it was missing."

"By golly, the horse paid off! Now I can put back the fifty I 'borrowed' from the till and have the hundred the horse made for me all to myself."

Of such dreams are embezzlements made. Bankers do it, stockbrokers do it; fathers, mothers and grandparents do it. Everybody has a bit of the embezzler in him.

Do lawyers embezzle? The shady ones do, and their group is growing. In this period of rising inflation, with the ratio of people to lawyers rapidly nearing a one-on-one situation, you'll see more embezzlement. It's frightening when one considers that of all the people who might embezzle and get away with it, the attorney is the least watched-over person alive when it comes to what he does with other people's moneys. The law requires that none of us embezzle, bar association codes of ethics require the same of all lawyers. In most instances neither the law nor the codes of ethics, command a lawyer to account for moneys entrusted to him. Thus he has more *chance* to embezzle than does another businessman because no one is around to keep an eye on him. There are no daily accountings of cash, familiar to every beleaguered bank teller, no weekly or monthly accountings. Nothing. When the client's case finally ends he *may* have to account but, who knows, that may be ten years from now!

Other people's money comes to lawyers by many different routes: court cost deposits, proceeds from the cash settlement of cases, cash portions of estates in probate matters, real estate purchase moneys, to name a few. The Code of Ethics requires that these funds be placed in a trustee-for-clients account by the attorney. Here he holds clients' moneys separate and apart from his own.

Most lawyers hew to the requirements of the Code of Ethics and don't meddle with their trust account moneys. How about those who do meddle?

* * *

b) Embezzlement of large sums of money

Contrary to popular belief, lawyers are human. Each is as vulnerable to the vagaries of temptation as any other citizen. Law schools train lawyers to resist temptation, and then the codes of ethics under which they operate help keep them in line. Most lawyers *can* resist temptation when it comes to other people's monies. Whether this is because they are ethical to the core, or because a large enough sum has never come along to tempt them, is not easy to discover. Which came first, the chicken or the egg?

During the 200-plus years of America's history there have been many thousands of cases of the embezzlement by lawyers of their clients' funds. All are similar, only the patterns differ. No state in our Union is without such cases and each of you has read of them in your local newspapers. Records of proceedings against these lawyers are also available for public scrutiny in state bar association offices across the land. But it is our purpose here to discuss these patterns of embezzlement, the cases in which they occur and how they occur. Grouped under several headings may be many thousands of cases, each with a different cast of characters but the same story, the same ending—the lawyer took from his client that which the client had entrusted to him.

The earlier discussed zeroing-in games and criminal law fee games are rarely reported because the client never knows he is involved in a game. Likewise, not all embezzlements are reported since often the lawyer, or any other trustee, has spent the money but managed to pay it back before the loss was discovered. By and large, however, the embezzler is caught far more often than the man who zeroes in on a bank account or charges exhorbitant fees. The Day of Reckoning finally arrives: the client wants his money. The lawyer either has it or he does not.

The probate of estates offers the most lucrative opportunities for embezzlement. Someone dies leaving an estate. The heirs see a lawyer concerning probate of the will or a probate-without-will. But the attorney is not the only party needed in a probate. An executor (in case of a will) or an administrator (if there is no will) must be appointed. The job of the executor or administrator is to round up all of the assets in the estate and hold same pending distribution by the court. This will include gathering cash from bank accounts, selling stock and real estate, collecting rents and dividends, and a myriad tasks all concerned with corraling assets and getting the estate in shape for eventual distribution of these assets. It's a tough job. More than likely the executor named in the will, or the administrator appointed by the court will be a friend or relative of the dead person. If it doesn't become apparent to him immediately, then not long after taking over such duties, the new executor will be as bewildered as Alice was in Wonderland, for the job he took leads through a frightening maze of rules, laws and tax regulations and reports. Nine times out of ten this relative or friend executor or administrator will turn to the lawyer for help.

The lawyer is glad to help. He cannot get his fee until the estate has closed. He wants to speed it along so that he can get paid. Having helped many an executor over the years he will generally know more about their duties than they do. In most states he does their work without additional pay. Legally he is only "helping them out." He doesn't mind, his extra work speeds up the case and the fee awaiting him at the end of the probate maze may be a large one.

The accounts of the executor are turned over to the lawyer as a part of such an undertaking. This saves the executor the trouble of having to sign checks and deposit money. The lawyer does it all in a special, trustee-for-client account which he alone controls.

Most lawyers run estates through probate faithfully and honestly, hewing to the ethics of their trade. It is the *un*ethical lawyer who concerns us. Their numbers are on the increase in every community. Hard pressed for money these lawyers will soon find that, in doing an executor's work, lucrative opportunities for continuing embezzlements await them.

The primary reason that the probate field offers the best over all chance for embezzlements is that it takes probate matters a long, long time to close. Smaller estates may be wound up within a year. These seldom interest the embezzling lawyer. Larger estates, however, may go on for many years. The "Jarndyce Estate" which Charles Dickens wrote of in *Bleak House*, ran through several generations. In such matters time becomes the ally of the probate attorney. Final distribution of the estate may be years away and interim accountings are only so much paperwork.

Temptation begins haunting the probate lawyer when moneys begin to rapidly accumulate in an estate. Stocks, homes, autos, bonds and other properties are sold. The cash goes into the special bank account. At the time of the first accounting to the court, for example, there may be, on paper some $250,000 in cash, with more to come. The devil within him, temptation, begins working on the mind of the lawyer.

Robert L. passed his state bar examinations at the same time I did in 1949. From a pre-bar exam course we had taken I learned he was a brilliant man. By the 1950s the legal and local newspapers were carrying stories of big cases that he was handling. I heard from time to time, from lawyers practicing in his area, that he was doing very well financially. Then in the early 1970s he got involved in a probate matter. The administratrix asked him to handle her end of the proceedings. In doing so, Robert, as trustee, came into possession of the proceeds of a sale of real property and of a pension fund. Temptation won the battle. He retained the proceeds himself, deposited only a portion of them in his trustee account and never repaid the balance to the estate. The administratrix complained to the state bar and Robert was disbarred from the practice of law by the Supreme Court. Interestingly enough, the proceedings before the bar brought out the fact that he had been suspended from practice for a period of six months in 1974 for having received moneys from a client to be applied towards a judgment that the client owed, and then not depositing the moneys to his trust account for two and a half years!

Robert's case is typical of the many thousands over the years that have involved embezzlement from estates. The clue to the Big Secret is that the attorney can always report to the court or client *on paper* as to what he is holding in money, when, in reality, he has already spent much of the money. Naturally, he hopes to pay it back before the estate closes. He knows that that may take a long time, but he has plenty of time. As in Robert's case, however, estates often close sooner than the attorney can replace the money. Temptation then goes a-scurrying while fear replaces it. The game is over, the jig is up.

Withdrawing funds from trust accounts, or not placing them there at all, is an easy matter. The courts do not want to look at passbooks, and they are content with what the attorney tells them, under oath, in writing. Strangely enough, few executors or administrators who are letting the attorney do their work for them ever ask to see passbooks either; they too are satisfied with the under-oath writing.

The attorneys not caught embezzling from estates will sometimes invest the money in sound stocks or other ventures, reap their profits, and replace the original amounts in their trust accounts. When the estate closes, the money is paid over, intact to the heirs, per court order.

But all too often the attorney will use his trustee money on unsafe ventures and only hope he can recoup for the pay-back. Practicing law is a matter of eternal hope—that *this* may be the day the big case will come into the office. Using that hope as a springboard the attorney may venture into the probate trust account, wander out with moneys not belonging to him and start spending.

Some attorneys are fairly certain that they will be able to replace the moneys. Some years ago a young attorney in my area took a sum (which I recall as being $6,000) from his trustee account to bet on the ponies at Santa Anita. He loved betting on races and plunged the money into several "sure things." The horses ran out of the money, so to speak. But our young man was saved! A few days later about $8,000 came into his trustee account from another source. He replaced the missing six. The balance of $2,000 was placed on the noses of some great racehorses. Unfortunately, on the day they ran for our young embezzler, they finished up down the track again. More money came into the trust account and more was spent trying to recoup the $8,-000. As time went on, other amounts were withdrawn in order to make money at Santa Anita. By the time the law caught up with this attorney he was down by about $14,000, money taken from several clients. The Supreme Court, in state bar proceedings, disbarred him from the practice of law.

The temptation may be to "keep up with the Joneses." Leading a social life as a lawyer is a tough proposition. You rub shoulders with wealthy lawyers (most of whom have married or inherited money) and keeping up with them is financially burdensome. If you have no money of your own then the dragged-out probate in the Makemunny case provides the trustee account from which to take it. You'll pay it back. The big case will come in that will repay it. Usually it doesn't come in and the state bar disbars another lawyer. Probate is great but leads too many lawyers astray.

Personal injury settlements, or any money damage settlements in civil lawsuits, provide another avenue of embezzlement for the attorney. The trouble here is that the time is usually short. The attorney embezzling such moneys for himself must replace them far sooner than the probate attorney would be required to. The client will normally know when the case is settled. Since most of these cases are settled by draft rather than check, the attorney may rightly tell him that the money can't be collected for possibly two weeks or, stretching the truth a bit, for a month. A draft is not payable on demand like a check but must be sent to the bank on which it is drawn for acceptance. Invariably the bank is out of town. That bank "accepts" it and then sends the proceeds of the draft to the lawyer's bank to be placed (hopefully!) in his trust account. This gives the unethical, embezzling attorney several weeks in which to operate. Sometimes he gets the money back in, sometimes not. There are thousands of "not" cases in the annals of bar association disciplinary proceedings.

A safer route to embezzlement in the collection of damages cases (whose proceeds always come through the lawyer in his capacity as agent for his client) is for the client to sign a waiver form. With such a form the client signs away his right to see and endorse the settlement check when it arrives, giving his attorney blanket power to sign in his place; the power sometimes extends to the signing of releases. The purpose of this, as explained to the client, is simple: it saves him having to come to the attorney's office to sign the settlement draft. Thus, in such situations, the client will often not be aware that the case was settled and the money is in.

In many of the reported cases I have read, it has often been a matter of a year or two, and sometimes more, before the client starts asking questions and pressing the attorney for answers. If all has gone well for him, the attorney can pay at this point. If matters have gone awry then someone will eventually tell the client to contact the state bar association—and goodbye to another lawyer.

In short-term matters, cases in which the client knows the case has been settled, the lawyer must fall back on a stall game if he misuses the funds when they arrive at his office. He will think up every logical excuse in the world as to why the money hasn't arrived. Eventually he will repay it to the trustee account or the client, who, now *sure* that something fishy has been going on, rather than merely suspicious, will blow the whistle on him. Hail and farewell to another embezzler!

Real estate transactions also allow the ne'er-do-well attorney to enjoy the use of funds not his own. In these situations the moneys involved are usually large sums. Seeking more and more avenues of work to bolster lagging incomes caused by the pressure of too much competition, attorneys appear to be getting more heavily involved in two fields of real estate:

(a) holding the sale moneys for seller clients, or

(b) being the escrow holders for the funds involved in the sale.

The latter, escrow arrangement offers the embezzlement-minded attorney the greater chance to withdraw moneys from the escrow. Escrows for the sale of land, like probates, often drag on for a considerable length of time. The more complex the sale (or the more complex the attorney can make it), the longer it takes to close it. Unlike the embezzler who takes a million and runs, the lawyer-embezzler generally intends to repay the funds; the former can retire, the latter must keep practicing law. If found out he knows he can lose his license to practice, and many do.

Short-term real estate matters, where the proceeds of a sale are paid to the seller through his attorney's trust account, are akin to the embezzlement of moneys from a personal injury case settlement; the client will grow suspicious if the attorney doesn't act reasonably soon. When using the money for his own purposes the lawyer must have a fairly good idea as to how he can repay it in a short time. Perhaps borrowing the money from another trust account is his solution! This has been done, as witness our earlier mentioned pony-playing attorney.

Probate, civil damage matters and real estate deals do not, of course, encompass the entire field of possibility for the embezzlement of large sums by attorneys of little conscience. Any time an attorney receives large amounts of money to hold for others, the temptation to use it is there. We can only hope that the client isn't *you*!

* * *

c) Embezzlement of small sums

Into the hands of every attorney come small amounts of money to be used for "court costs"—court filing fees, services of process, reporters' costs on depositions, moneys for investigators and dozens of sundry odds and ends. These sums may be small in the case of one client, but they become large when one hundred clients or more are involved.

The consequences of wiping out his entire trustee-for-clients account in one fell swoop, when a hundred-plus clients are involved, are too serious for the smart embezzler. Unless he has a sure-fire way of repaying a great deal of the money almost immediately, he will soon be brought to task because of his failure to pay court costs. Some of his cases are starting, some are ending and most are in between. Court costs are therefore due in one case or another almost daily. The attorney can not stave them all off for the purpose of one grand embezzlement (unless his purpose is to retire forever!).

The unethical lawyer entrusted with small sums from hundreds of clients will, if he's in need of money, divert small amounts to his own use from time to time. When a cost payment becomes due he can pay it from the thousands of dollars lying in the trustee account.

He may be using Mary's dollar to pay Paul's costs, but neither will know for their moneys become as one when placed in the trustee account. Save for long-drawn-out matters involving large sums, or where the law may require it, it would be impossible to open a trust account for every client. Some clients have only one-time deposits of moneys that are spent in bang-bang fashion: sums for filing a lawsuit and the service of process on the defendant. Often no more court costs are entrusted to the lawyer in such cases.

One device used by most lawyers is to secure a lump sum in advance for "court costs to be used in the future." Rather than bill the client from time to time for this cost or that as it arises, the attorney can simply withdraw the sums from his trustee account as needed. Most never touch these sums for their own use. Those who do so can see the "beauty" of extracting, say, $500 in advance to be used for costs in a case that may drag out for several years. Often much of the money is used but just as often very little of it is. Sitting there, unused, it presents a temptation to the attorney who desperately needs a quick hundred or two. Why not take it? The client won't be asking questions until the case ends who knows how long from now. Why not repay the money on the long distant day when the lawsuit finally closes?

Attorneys are seldom prosecuted for the embezzlement of small sums, for the simple reason that they are rarely caught. They can wheel and deal along the way and always come up with the costs money when needed, even if it means borrowing to do so. An attorney of my acquaintance, who appeared wealthy, died suddenly. The probate of his estate turned up the fact that he was almost a million dollars in debt! Yet by wheeling and dealing he was successful by today's standards. Had he lived, no doubt he could have kept his facade of wealth intact for many years for he had learned the game well, and knew every trick involved in when to borrow, how to repay, who to keep at arm's length, who to pay back. His creditors and clients are still waiting.

Small-sum embezzlers are more easily caught when they fail to set up a trustee account and mingle clients' moneys with their own. The "commingling of an attorney's funds with those of his own" (usually in just one account) is a ground for disbarment from the practice of law. When there are not enough moneys in that account to pay the client what is due him, the client blows the whistle. During the state bar proceedings it will then be disclosed that the attorney had but one account. Disbarment often follows, although in many instances the attorney is only suspended until he repays the client—a sort of short jail sentence as compared to imprisonment for life. Many successfully get away with keeping money in one account because there is always enough money on hand. Who will then know the attorney keeps but one account? It is usually unforeseen problems that doom the commingling attorney. One lawyer whom I knew kept only one account for many years. He was honest as the day is long on June 21 in the northern hemisphere. Money due for court costs or to be repaid to clients was always promptly disbursed. The "unforeseen problem" that arose in his case stemmed from the demon rum. He started drinking heavily. Booze, like the ponies and behind-the-scenes girl friends, costs money. Soon the money is gone, and soon after that the clients start complaining. The strange thing about this man's case was that he was suspended three times from the practice of law, each time for having failed to set up a trustee account, and each time was reinstated. Each time he promised to set up a trustee account, and each time he didn't. In the end, on the fourth occasion he had to appear before the bar, he was disbarred from the practice of law. He was a likeable guy but just hated the bookkeeping that would be required with a trustee-for-clients account.

* * *

What you can do about embezzlement

1. In probate matters, where you are an executor or administrator but have turned these duties over to your attorney, ask for a look at his trustee account passbooks and monthly balance sheets from time to time. If he refuses then something may well be "rotten in the state of Denmark." The ethical attorney will have no qualms about agreeing and may even be pleased at your taking such an interest in a case where he is doing all of your work for which you, at probate's end, will be paying; he is hoping your interest may spark you into doing some of the work yourself!

2. In personal injury matters, never give attorneys blanket power to sign your name on checks or releases. Most attorneys are ethical, but how do you know yours is, or will be if the sum involved is a large one? It may take up a bit more time to go into his office to sign release papers and later to endorse the settlement draft, or to do it by mail, but doing so will protect you against possible embezzlement of *your* money.

To be sure, the "protection" spoken of is not absolute. If you know when it was that you endorsed the draft, however, you will have a pretty good idea as to when the money will be collected. Should you reside in New York and the settlement draft is drawn on a California bank, the attorney's bank will have it mailed to California for collection. Assuming four days for going and four days for coming and the drawee bank in California taking its own sweet time (as they always seem to do in cases involving large amounts), you can count on the money being back in the attorney's account in two weeks, three at the outside. If at the end of three weeks you haven't heard from him start calling every day (attorneys "love" the client who calls every day but it does make them start moving!). If he is still stalling you at the end of the month follow suggestion #4 below.

3. In all other matters involving large sums, whether in real estate deals, probate, personal injury or anything else, in situations where the attorney has the money, demand to see monthly checking account statements and, from time to time without announcement, to look at savings passbooks.* By keeping on top of the money you will keep it from straying into the attorney's own account. Why should you help to gratify his taste for wine, women and song?

4. Unlike Russia, the United States does not have a governmental *Division for the Struggle Against Embezzlement.* In Russia, the government owns all property so, of course, anyone who embezzles is taking from the government. In America, though the government is amassing more and more property each year, it doesn't own it all as yet!

Complaints should go to your state bar association or local district attorney. Should you have a solid suspicion that your attorney is fooling around with your money (did his secretary's new fur coat come from *your* trust account?) write immediately to the state bar, or if possible go there in person. Every state bar in the country is anxious to change the bad image lawyers have attained over the years. They know that the majority of lawyers are honest, hardworking, non-embezzling men and women. Knowing this they want to clean the barrel of its bad apples. More than ever before state bar associations are investigating and bringing to justice those of their number who are engaging in unethical practices. The embezzlement of funds belonging to clients is the misdeed most commonly found. Pursue your case with the state bar through to completion. If you drop charges, or don't complain at

---

*Where an attorney will be holding a rather large sum, certainly for a long period of time, he should deposit it in a savings account so that the client's money earns interest.

all, you are encouraging that "bad apple" to continue his nefarious conduct, allowing him to hurt others. Stay with it. Not only will you get your money back as a term of the sentence imposed on the lawyer but you may well stop him from playing games with other people's money.

CHAPTER 7

All Talk and No Action

"Take the Money and Run"

One of my finest experiences in lawyering took place before I passed my bar exams when I was working for a lawyer who procrastinated. He would always put off until the day after tomorrow, anything that could be done today. At least he eventually got the work done. Fine experience? You bet! It taught me the valuable lesson that a lawyer should start work on a client's case as soon as he is retained.

I hadn't been working for this fellow very long when a man came to the office one day to inquire how his divorce papers were coming along. The boss not being in, I pulled the file. All it held was an initial interview sheet dated almost two years before.

"Have you seen him since [naming the date]?" I inquired.

"No," was his reply. "He told me he'd call me when the papers were ready."

"Did you pay him a retainer?"

"No. He said I could pay when the papers were signed."

Whew! At least he hadn't taken the money and run.

The case finally got started but why the boss waited two years to start it, or why the client waited that long to check on his papers, was beyond me.

Since then I have learned that there are a goodly number of attorneys who drag their heels when it comes to getting around to working on cases in which they've been retained. These procrastinators are of both the honest and dishonest variety. The former includes my old boss. By nature he just never got around to things. The latter includes lawyers who take the money and, while hoping the client bothers them no further, do nothing at all. Strangely, there are many

85

clients who never check with the lawyer again or, as in the earlier example, wait a couple of years before doing so. In the case of the two-year wait to start a divorce my boss could have been in deep trouble with the bar association if he had taken a retainer at the initial conference. Taking a fee without working on the case within a reasonable time thereafter violates the Code of Ethics and, upon complaint to the bar association, is an actionable offense.

In the Matter of Selznick, a recent California case, the Supreme Court found conclusive evidence that the lawyer involved had taken a $1,000 retainer fee to handle an appeal but had never filed the appeal. The lawful time in which an appeal could be filed had gone by and the client was now barred forever from appealing the lower court's decision. Such cases are the worst of the lot in the "no action" game. By procrastinating, the attorney causes his clients to lose valuable rights, which in some cases they can never regain. Statutes of Limitation, periods within which matters must be filed, apply to every kind of case. When the retained attorney fails to file within the period prescribed by law he is guilty of unethical conduct.

Even though the time set by the Statute of Limitations may not have run out in a particular case, the attorney who delays filing a suit and thereafter pursuing it diligently to trial, may be seriously hurting his client in other ways. In The Matter of Cosgrove, the California Supreme Court found that the lawyer involved had commenced a probate matter but had done nothing more about it. Three years later the unhappy client contacted the state bar about it. An investigation turned up still another disgruntled client; in the second case the attorney had taken no action for twenty-eight months even though the suit involved title to a valuable piece of real estate. In each case the lawyer had taken the money (the retainer) and "sat on his hands."

Tarrying too long to file your personal injury case often results in the disappearance of key witnesses, the changing of landmarks at the scene of the accident, and the fading of memories in those witnesses, and participants, who remain. All of this waiting hurts your case. More greatly hurt, of course, is the client whose lawyer fails to file the case within the period of the Statute of Limitations. This client has forever lost a chance to sue. Today more and more of these clients are suing their attorneys for malpractice. A born procrastinator should never enter the field of law. In law *time* is always an important factor.

The "waiting time record" would appear to be held by an attorney who for eight years ignored an estate he was retained to handle. Why the client waited that long to complain will never be known, but the attorney involved received a verbal, public "spanking" by the court. He was not disbarred because the client had lost nothing, moneywise, by reason of the delay.

A new game in the "no action" field has resulted from the free legal services which various governments, local, state and federal, provide for those unable to afford the services of an attorney. The services may be free to the client but the government must pay attorneys to handle these matters for the poor. Though I had heard that the new game existed, I did not know it did for certain until the U.S. government indicted a Los Angeles attorney for turning in seventy-three false claims for services he claimed to have rendered to indigent clients, but which he hadn't rendered at all. It now appears certain that such goings-on are occurring all over the country, primarily in large urban areas. Here we have the "double hurt" situation: clients who ask for help and don't get it, and tax payers who pay for services attorneys never render.

Those attorneys who engage in the "all talk and no action game" are often hard to ferret out. In every lawsuit (aside from criminal cases) there are occasions when long periods of time will go by without any ac-

tion by the attorney being necessary. A trial date
secured by him may, for example, be two or three
years away. During this time, aside from depositions,
medical examinations and the concluding of investigations, there is nothing in which the client will be
directly involved. Timewise, it would be prohibitive
for the attorney to call or write every client, every
week, to say "Nothing's new." While the civil and
probate court systems do move slowly as a matter of
fact, a growing number of lawyers are using this as an
excuse for their own inaction. They blame delay on
the system when, in truth, it is their lack of initiative
that is holding cases up in many instances. They
feather their own nests with retainer fees. Thereupon
they sit in the nest and take no action.

* * *

What you can do about all talk and no action

1. In criminal matters you have little to worry
about in the "no action" field. At the outset of a case
the police or clerk of the court will advise you of your
first appearance day in court. Thereafter you will be
notified by the clerk of the next date. If your attorney
is late, or doesn't show up at all, he will be severely
admonished by the judge. Since lawyers invariably
want to stay on the good side of judges in criminal matters (because, in the end, they advise most of their
clients to plead "guilty" and thus prefer a judge who,
at least, doesn't dislike them), this won't happen too
often. Criminal lawyers have their own "games," as
discussed earlier, and procrastination is generally not
a habit practiced by them.

2. Iron out "time" problems with your attorney
during the first interview. Find out just what is involved, courtwise, from start to finish; determine the
approximate time-lapses that will occur between every

stage of the case. A client in a divorce case, after addressing her queries to her attorney at their first conference, might be told the following:

> I will have your Complaint/Petition and other papers ready for you to read and sign in four or five days. A day or two after that I will file them with the court; the first Order to Show Cause hearing will come up in fifteen to twenty days after the case is filed; I will immediately have my secretary advise you of the date. After that hearing the case can go in one of two directions: first, if your husband does not secure an attorney and fight the case we can take his default 30 days after he was served. When taking his default we also file a request that the matter be set down for the divorce hearing. I find out a week or two after filing exactly what the date is. I then notify you of it. The only "kicker" here insofar as time is concerned, is that your husband may get a lawyer to aid him in settling the case. If chances of settling appear favorable we may waive the thirty-day time limit for defaults so as to secure a settlement. If it appears to me, though, that they are stalling, or that we are permanently log-jammed on some issue or other, we will ask them to contest the case, giving them ten or fifteen days in which to do so. If they do contest the case by filing the proper papers, the attorney should file all papers necessary to set the case down for trial. Contested divorces in our courts are generally taking a year to get to trial. When I know the exact date I will let you know.

From such an interview you have secured a rough idea of the time periods involved. If, after a week, you haven't heard from the attorney who was to have your papers ready to sign "in four or five days," call him to see what the problem is. If he gives you no specific date for coming in to sign, then call him daily. Daily calls from a client drive lawyers crazy. However, such calls do get the slow ones moving, if only to stop the daily calling!

If, after signing, you don't hear from the attorney for a week, call him again. Remember that he told you

that he would file your papers a day or two after you
signed them and that a preliminary court date would
be given to him at that time. A call to your attorney
will determine

(a) whether he's filed the case and, if so,

(b) when the hearing date is. If he hasn't filed suit
call him daily until he does so.

A week or so after the hearing contact your attorney
again to learn whether or not your husband has
retained an attorney. If he has not done so then ask
your attorney to file a default as soon as the thirty-day
waiting period expires. Should your husband have
secured an attorney, have your own counsel keep you
posted on developments. If, after a lapse of a month or
so without news of the case, you grow concerned (as
you should), call your attorney to find out what's up.
If nothing has happened tell him to start things
happening. Should he have fallen into the trap of
waiting for the other attorney to do something, tell him
in no uncertain terms to get off the dime and move
matters toward a trial date. Thereafter a weekly call to
your attorney will keep things rolling.

3. *Stay "on top" of your case at all times.* If there
are time lags, find out why they are occurring. Should
you have a suspicion that your lawyer has not filed the
lawsuit, or the necessary trial-setting papers, or other
items he claims he is going to file, ask him bluntly
whether he's done them. If you still doubt his word go
to the courthouse, ask to see your court file, and find
out if your attorney has been leveling with you.

Whether you're suing for money, injunctions,
damages, divorce or anything else, your case *is* important. Take the time to find out what's going on. Should
your lawyer be defending an action for you, make certain all papers necessary to defend the action have
been filed with the court.

The odds favor your securing an ethical lawyer who
will move your case right along. There is an ever-
growing chance, however, that he may fall into the

other category of attorney. If he's an "all talk and no action" lawyer, you may find yourself in deep trouble.

CHAPTER 8

The Low Settlement Game

Anne was a plaintiff in a personal injury case. While driving down a freeway her auto had been rear-ended by a vehicle traveling considerably faster than hers. She suffered a concussion with loss of consciousness, a severe cerebral contusion and painful back injuries. With these she had the first two of the three elements necessary for a *good* personal injury case: the severe injuries and the liability on the part of the other driver.

She stayed in the hospital two weeks. Six weeks later she was released by her doctor. By then she had amassed some $3,500 in medical bills and lost wages. These were her "special damages," an item which usually goes hand in hand with the settlement evaluation of personal injury cases.

By that time the third element of a good lawsuit—financial responsibility on the part of the other driver*—had been established. An experienced personal injury attorney would have evaluated her case as being worth a minimum of $15,000 at that point.

But there is always a fourth element lurking in every injury suit: the attorney the plaintiff selects. Anne had selected her lawyer in the following manner: the friend of a friend of a friend of hers knew about this "neat" attorney. Anne, knowing no attorneys, selected him solely on this recommendation. And he *was* a neat guy—young, personable, handsome and intelligent. His only drawback (which Anne didn't know about) was that he had only been in private practice a very short time. She was also unaware that he was hard up

---

*"Financial responsibility" normally means that the other party has auto insurance to cover injury he has caused others. Those who don't have insurance are generally those who can't afford it. They are seldom sued because if a judgment is secured against them they promptly go into bankruptcy.

for money, having plunged all he had into his swanky new offices. His income, as is the case with most young attorneys, was on the lean and hungry side.

For Anne this fourth element of her personal injury case proved a disaster. The day after her doctor released her the neat attorney she had retained urged her to accept a $5,000 settlement. He based his "take it, baby" argument on the fact that while in the ambulance, on the way to the hospital after the accident, Anne's ambulance attendant swore that he'd heard her mumble that the accident was her fault. "Incredible!" thought Anne. She knew the fault was not hers. As a nurse she also knew that people in shock and suffering from concussion are apt to say anything. The attorney, however, pressed on. The whole case, he told her, now rode on the ambulance attendant's statement. If a jury believed him she would get nothing. Completely neglecting the salient fact—how did the accident happen?—he prevailed on her to accept the $5,000. What, after all, did she know about the legal aspects of personal injury suits?

From the $5,000 settlement Anne's attorney deducted his one third fee (for three months "work.") What was left to her was $3,333, an amount less than the total of all of her bills and lost wages. She was still out of pocket about $167 on a case many lawyers dream of getting because of the high settlement potential.

Her own insurance agent (whose advice she had not sought) was flabbergasted. He assured her that the case was worth far more than $5,000. An experienced personal injury attorney whom she *then* saw advised her that the case had a minimum value of at least $15,-000. He recommended she complain to the state bar. She did so.* A legal malpractice case was also in the

---

*The bar, unfortunately, did nothing for Anne. They classed her attorney's low settlement as an "error in judgment" on his part. The bar's staff, they explained, was not large enough to handle complaints in this area. It's true that the bar is inundated these days with complaints in fields they consider more serious—embezzlement,

offing. She would have been wiser to have contacted her local bar association to select a lawyer specializing in these cases.

In a damage suit—personal injury or otherwise—every case has an eventual settlement value. This value is, for the most part, predicated on liability. In an excellent case of liability (you're 100 percent "in the right") your case is worth what insurance people call "top dollar." Should the other party have defenses that weaken the case, it is worth proportionately less. It is the attorney's job to appraise the value of each case. Ability to appraise comes only through experience. The young attorney, handling his first case or two, should always seek outside advice from older lawyers or personal friends in the insurance field in pursuing the *true value* of his case. Neither his empty stomach nor his deficit bank account should control his decision to settle. In Anne's matter the lawyer earned $1666.66, a goodly sum for anyone and especially for a young, starving attorney. Should a client's case be so poor that the probabilities rule against his recovering his medical bills and lost wages from a settlement or verdict, then the lawyer should either not take the case or should reduce his fee so that the client at least breaks even. Lawyering is a service for the benefit of clients and for the lawyer's benefit only after the client has been satisfied. Anne's lawyer, in our example, was apparently too proud to seek outside help or advice. How much each year is lost because of pride!

Whereas Anne had no opinion as to the value of her case, many clients seem inclined to over-evaluate the damage actions they bring to a lawyer. Remember the example, earlier mentioned, of the horsefly in the Coke bottle. The client's $10,000 price tag for that one was far beyond reality. Well-meaning friends, neigh-

---

ambulance chasing and other games you are reading about in this book—but it's to be hoped that some day its staff will be able to help in Anne's type of case.

bors and relatives lead many of these over-evaluators astray; each has some case to relate, a case *"just like yours,"* in which some extravagant sum was secured by settlement or verdict. A newspaper rewrite man might caption a story, MAN GETS $50,000 FOR BROKEN LEG, stress the bum leg in the story and cut out portions concerning disc injuries to the back. Insurance company adjusters are specialists trained in determining the value of a personal injury case, and so are lawyers who dwell primarily in that field.

A client may visit a lawyer with the preconceived notion that his case is worth $25,000. After carefully studying the facts the lawyer-specialist advises him it has a value of around $5,000. The client leaves. Searching long enough he may find a lawyer who will assure this client that the case *is* worth $25,000. Either the lawyer doesn't know any better or he figures that somehow he can eventually prevail on the client to take something around five. Keep on lookin'. Eventually you'll find someone who will agree with anything you say. Or would you rather know the truth?

The trouble with the "low settlement game" is that the affliction is not always confined to the young inexperienced attorney. Older ones have been known to settle at too low a figure, and older attorneys playing at this game are hard for the client to recognize. The kindly gray-haired lawyer, sitting in his plush office, may well have the experience to know what a case is worth, and perhaps he has. How is the client to know, though, that his wife is divorcing him and it is costing him heavily, that business has been slow and he is hard up for dollars, that yesterday he lost everything he had in a stock market slump, that he has a mistress whose financial demands are getting out of hand? The lawyer is not going to tell you any of this. You can be suspicious that something is amiss, however, when he takes the case, presses for a quick settlement and then advises you to take the first offer the other party makes. Better lawyers bargain awhile until they get an offer they feel is satisfactory. Rarely does an insurance carrier offer exactly what you feel the case is worth. They bargain too.

A subliminal game which attorneys, young and old, may play in damages cases, personal injury or otherwise, revolves around the word "reasonable." Every case should be settled for its reasonable value. Webster calls "reasonable" something that is "agreeable to reason . . . not extreme or excessive." You use the word every day.

"Sirloin steak is $1.79 a pound this week," your butcher tells you.

"That's reasonable," you answer, remembering that down the street it sells for $2.09 while last year it was going for $1.49.

Somewhere in between high and low, somewhere between good and bad, there's "reasonable."

Lawyers first come upon the word early in law school. The law, they find, falls back on the word "reasonable" whenever it fails to come up with an exact definition. It speaks of what a "reasonable man would do under the circumstances" in many situations. In courses on damages, the sum and substance of evaluating the worth of civil cases is that the settlement or jury award must be reasonable. The word means everything, and it means nothing, for in and of itself it presents no guidelines.

Once an attorney has gained experience in the civil damages field he learns that there are three shades of the word involved in the evaluation of the case: high, middle and low reasonable. The former is considered the "top dollar" value of the case—what a jury might award should you go to trial or what you might extract by way of settlement on the courthouse steps. "Low reasonable" is sometimes what the carrier first offers, sometimes something just above this. As long as the attorney stays within the bounds of "reasonable" he is safe from chastisement from the state bar.

"It is a bit low, but it's within reason," one experienced lawyer may say of another's settlement.

The lawyer, earlier referred to, who settled a

minimum-value $15,000 case for the first offer of
$5,000 seems well outside the limits of "reasonable."

So we come to the word "subliminal." It suggests,
as is in fact the case, that the attorney's subconscious
is controlling his decisions. It is a game, then, that is
played without either lawyer or client knowing a game
is involved. Only the attorney's subconscious knows.
By way of example, the game would go something like
this:

The attorney is getting older. He has tried many a
personal injury case and with great success. Lately,
however, he feels weary after the trial of such a case.
He chalks this up to increasing age. His subconscious,
however, is saying, "I don't like trials anymore.
They're a bore. Make more settlements and go to trial
less."

An offer of settlement is made. His conscious mind
tells him it's low but reasonable, his subconscious
yearns to take it. The attorney comes back with a
counter-offer. Strangely, the counter-proposal for settlement is lower than one he might have made even a
year ago. His subconscious is pressing. Eventually
he'll settle in the middle range or perhaps in that un-
definable territory between low and middle. The settlement, in any event, is "reasonable."

The client, not knowing (as most don't) the value of
the case, finds the settlement acceptable. The lawyer's
conscience may bother him for a little while (he sus-
pects he could have made more by holding out or going to trial) but when, in the next case, he follows the
same pattern his conscience fades under the onslaught
of the subconscious. Clients sometimes lose many
dollars through this "game," but while a few suspect
they are doing so, far fewer know it for a fact. Charges
against a lawyer for settling "too low" would not
carry weight with the bar. His settlements were in the
range of "reasonable."

* * *

What can you do about the low settlement game

1. Call your local bar association to obtain a referral to an attorney who specializes in the damages field into which your case falls—auto accident, workmen's compensation, slip and fall, probate, real property losses, or whatever it may be. If your bar association does not list lawyers by specialities of practice, then search among your friends for one who has had a case in the field of your present complaint. If he was satisfied with the results his lawyer got, then go to his attorney.

2. Try not to select an attorney at random unless it is a minor matter you feel any lawyer could handle. I repeat, do not use the yellow pages name lists to select a lawyer (as a novice might pick a horse to win a race because of its pretty name) because you are chancing everything on Lady Luck. This grand old dame, as you well know, is a fickle sort and with her it's often "Heads I win, tails you lose."

Lest the yellow pages at this juncture start making plans to sue me for defamation of their sterling character, let me say that I do a lot of walking through these pages myself. On such a walk you'll learn a lot, but only if you remember that it comes primarily from the advertisements, which are no more reliable than other advertisements. Herein lies the reason for not *choosing* a lawyer from the yellow pages list. Your bar association, however, is reliable, so check with them. The advantage of the yellow pages as opposed to the white is that once you have an attorney's name, they make it easier to find his address and phone number; the yellows will often carry the lawyer's suite number as well, whereas the whites often do not.

Every New Year's Eve I contemplate the fact that ninety percent of the next year's income will be from things that haven't even happened yet—an accident, a death, a divided home, a burglary. A gruesome thought, but true. Among my clients-to-be, I know there will be several who picked me simply because they liked my name and for that reason alone!

In what I now look back on as my "heyday" (modest as it was), I primarily handled auto accident and divorce cases. These, taken together, represent the vast majority of cases filed in any state. Thus it follows that most of the persons selecting my name had matters in these particular fields. But it was just a matter of blind luck. Those whose cases fell into fields of law I rarely handled, if at all, I referred out to attorneys who I knew were competent in such fields. Most attorneys will do this. Larger firms generally have attorneys operating in every specialty, so someone in these offices will take your case.

3. I can only hope I don't stir up the wrath of very new, very young attorneys by rule #3. Such is not my intent. Many, if not most of them, may have I.Q.'s that are higher than mine. Yet in this chapter we are speaking of the evaluation of damages for the purpose of settlement. Experience in the field is, I feel, far more important than knowledge of the law. Knowledge takes care of one aspect of a case, to wit, liability, but matching liability with the injuries and bills involved comes from having more than a few cases under one's belt. If the lawyer you eventually visit appears quite young ask him:

(a) When he was admitted to practice in your state, and

· (b) about how many cases of your type he has had. If he lies about either or both and later settles for what you consider "beans" you will have a stronger case against him with the bar association. Should he seem "too new" to you, you can always walk out. If you want him, anyway, ask if he will, when settlement time rolls around, seek the advice of an older attorney, experienced in this field, before settling. Most older ones are glad to help the younger ones. The young attorney who is repelled by the idea of seeking outside counsel is one of whom you should be wary. There are none of us so smart we don't need the advice of others once in a while!

4. Many persons involved in personal injury damages suits wait until they are well and/or discharged from their doctor's care before seeing an attorney. Don't! The attorney who gets a case from the outset has the advantage. Witnesses' memories are still fresh and they are still around. There are police reports, doctors' reports and medical bills to secure. All of these things must be done before settlement can be even remotely considered. The attorney can be doing these things while you are getting well. When you are well he may be ready to settle. If at that stage you are seeing him for the first time, he must start from scratch and valuable time will be lost.

5. The only defense against the games the attorney will play with you in settlement matters, be they conscious games of settling for too little or the subliminal game of settling too soon, is to apply your own logic and common sense to settlement offers when made. If they sound too small and you are convinced they are, hold out. The client's interests, not the lawyer's, come first.

CHAPTER 9

Advertising

Yesterday

Many years ago when, as a young lawyer, I was a member of the Board of Directors of my local bar association, a great portion of one meeting was devoted to a new lawyer in town who had had the audacity to have his name printed in block letters fourteen inches high, on his office window. The Code of Ethics at that time limited the size of such lettering to eight inches, as I remember. Memory fades as one grows older. Perhaps the legal size was ten or twelve and this lawyer's lettering was sixteen or eighteen inches in height. The difference, anyway, was about six inches.

Any lettering above the height required by the code was "advertising" and advertising was unlawful. In this particular case the lettering size seemed doubly unlawful because this lawyer's office happened to be across the street from the city jail. He thought, I imagine (and I imagine he was right), that prisoners standing at the jailhouse window could better see his name if it were a little larger. As there were several lawyers located across the street from the jail he wanted the inmates to see his name first. Bordering the black letters in red also aided the prisoners who gazed outward toward his office.

After a long debate on the matter the board finally decided that, rather than immediately admonish the lawyer in question, they would direct the secretary to send him a letter of warning. He was to remove the lettering and come up with something of legal size within two weeks. If he failed to do this the issue would be turned over to the state bar.

The effect of the letter must have scared the newcomer half to death, for when I went by his offices about ten days later the lettering was gone completely and his office was empty. He had left town, seeking, no doubt, a smaller town whose bar knew a little less than ours about minor points of legal ethics.

I thought the issue somewhat petty. But as we had only one other matter to discuss that particular noontime, to wit, "Should the local bar association endorse the sale of Girl Scout cookies?" our time had to be spent in some meaningful fashion. Nowadays, our board meetings last two hours, cover a variety of complex issues and the secretary, on word from the president, automatically sends out letters of warning to those who are violating smaller points of legal ethics, the size of lettering or whatever.

The name(s) of the person or persons who first decided that attorneys-at-law should not advertise have long been forgotten, if they were ever recorded. As far back as one likes to go in the history of legal ethics it seems impossible to discover the point at which advertising was first banned. England was our mother country and we have drawn much of our law and standards from her. The practice of law in England was considered a dignified profession (particularly amongst those who practiced it) and advertising seemed beneath the dignity of the barrister or solicitor. It was true then as now, that lawyers had "runners" and these business seekers were, in effect, the ad-men for the profession. Runners were discussed in greater detail in the chapters on ambulance chasing. However, Madison Avenue concepts in advertising have always been a no-no in the profession. Even the most fraudulent of shysters turned his back on the idea of out-and-out advertising so long as the no-advertising rule remained on the books.

Yesterday lawyers "advertised" by getting their names in the papers or on radio.

"It doesn't matter how they spell your name or mispronounce it," one older lawyer told me when I first set up in practice, "as long as people know it's *you* they're talking about."

By entering politics, joining clubs or starting crusades, lawyers always ensured that their names were mentioned in newsprint or on the air. Lawyers joined churches and P.T.A.'s and more than a few have turned to preaching the Gospel as ministers—simply or mainly to pass the word that they were practicing law. With the advent of television, lawyers have sought, and often found, ways and means of getting their faces on the tube; then, somewhere in the program, is mentioned the fact that they are in the lawyering business. The program *host* mentions this, of course, for the lawyer fears the state bar may start chasing him if he talks too much about his practice.

Better lawyers have always depended primarily on word of mouth from satisfied clients to secure business. This remains the tried and tested, age-old method of securing clients. One client tells two others, they in turn each tell two more and so the clientele pyramid is built. In five years or ten, a lawyer has built a law practice. Many are the notable lawyers in every city and town in America who are unknown to those who live outside their narrow area of operation. They have been and will continue to be successful only because of word of mouth.

So we move toward today. In the yesterdays of law the "ad games" a lawyer might play with the public were primarily limited to overexposure in the newspapers, the result of which might be that this layman or that believed Lawyer A was a good lawyer when in fact he was not. The lack of advertising may well have hurt the general public because, not knowing lawyers to whom they should go, and perhaps not having a bar association that listed lawyers by their specialties, its only recourse was the hit-or-miss method of looking up names in a phone book. Which one specialized in the type of case the potential client had? There was no way of knowing. Hit or miss, take your chances.

Today

Fiercely blow the winds of change.

Added now to the younger lawyers and the fringe group who have always wanted to advertise, are older, established lawyers who are beginning to feel the pinch of competition. The addition of this group is significant in the move toward change for it is these lawyers, the established, upper echelon attorneys, who have long controlled state and local bar associations. If they decide that change is necessary it will come about.

California, turning out more new lawyers per capita than any other state in the union each year, is succumbing to the pressures to allow advertising. Other states are following suit and by 1980 probably all fifty states will have fallen into line. As of this writing California has allowed lawyers specializing in taxation, criminal law and workmen's compensation to advertise that they are specialists in these fields. To become a "specialist" under current rules is, however, no easy matter. A lawyer holding himself out as a criminal law specialist, for example, must get the okay of the state bar. To get this approval he must have engaged in twenty jury trials, taken sixty hours of "outside courses"* relating to criminal law, and satisfied several other requirements including a minimum of five years in the practice of law. Thus a layman seeing a lawyer listed in the yellow pages as a "criminal law specialist" will know what he is getting; the same is true for those listed as taxation and workmen's comp.

---

*The California State Bar sponsors a continuing education program which features several lectures each month in criminal law and other fields. It is these and related courses, not law school courses, to which this sixty-hour stipulation applies.

specialists. Legal directories, now published by consumer, labor, business and professional groups are also allowed to include such specializations after the attorney's name.

The pressure continues. Lawyers in the divorce, personal injury, collections and other fields want to advertise as specialists as well. They will, within the year, succeed. The state bar will set up guidelines (such as those for criminal law specialists mentioned above) for allowing them to commence advertising their own specialties. The pressure won't end here. Lawyers who have been in practice less than five years, added to those who have a "general practice" with no particular specialty, will soon dominate the bar. It seems easy to predict that by 1980 they will force the issue of advertising to the point that they, not the bar, will decide the fields in which they wish to advertise. The gates will then be open and we might find ads such as these:

> HENRY DRAKE, attorney at law
> General practice in *all* fields of law.
> (address/phone #)
> ROGER TAKEMALL, attorney at law
> *Specializing in:*
> Criminal Law
> Workmen's Compensation
> Personal Injury cases
> Probate
> Divorce
> Collections
> Oil and Gas Law
> Corporations
> Adoptions
> Wills
> Civil (both plaintiff and defense)
> Juvenile Court matters
> (Address and phone numbers)

That Roger didn't name *every* field of law would probably be the result of his not wanting to appear greedy. The fact that he had opened his law office just a month previously would not be mentioned.

Now lawyers are beginning to play games again. Without state bar sanctions for specialties, how will the public know the attorneys it selects are really, truly, died-in-the-wool specialists in any field? What will become of the true criminal law specialist who now finds every other lawyer in the yellow pages listing himself as a criminal law specialist? Young lawyers, especially, want to become criminal lawyers. Those overabundant crime shows on TV are often what spur them to become real-life Perry Masons.

With the advent of state bar certified specialists in several fields, the advertising door has opened. The eventual allowing of each lawyer to pick his own specialty will open the door even wider. It won't end there. Once a door is open the person on the threshold can witness the glories that lie in the room beyond. Specialization announcements are child's play compared to the advertising Land of Oz that awaits the lawyer of the future.

Advertising by lawyers has now reached the same state that federal income tax found itself in in 1912. The income tax amendment passed in that year pegged income tax at 2 percent (2 percent!); this is equivalent to the bar allowing *some* advertising.

When federal income tax was finally pushed through, Senator Borah of Idaho suggested (God bless his soul!) that a ceiling of ten percent on income tax be included in the new law. He was shushed to silence by those who suggested that, if such a ceiling were placed on the tax, it would give someone upstairs the idea of raising taxes to ten percent!

"Just keep quiet about it," he was told in effect, "and income tax will stay at two and then probably be forgotten."

As federal income tax today rapidly approaches a 100 percent ceiling, some of the moans you hear are coming from the ghost of the later Senator Borah. The others are from the ghosts of lawyers who deplored the bar's opening of the advertising door. Their moans will become louder, however, because they ain't seen nothin' yet!

Tomorrow

A young lawyer is suing the New York City Bar Association in Federal District Court. His claim is that the bar's failure to allow him to advertise is costing him several millions of dollars in lost business. His suit will undoubtedly be lost if only because the court would, in allowing *his* case to stand, be allowing the 450,000 lawyers in our country to likewise sue their respective bar associations for billions of dollars.

This lawsuit is but the beginning. Young lawyers and not-so-good lawyers are restive. Their pocketbooks are hurting. Lawyers, as advertisers, will put Madison Avenue hucksters to shame. Lawyers have always been thwarted actors and admen. They find an outlet for their thespian talents in jury trials, but they will soon have their day as admen as newspapers, radio, TV and office fronts give them the chance to display their wares.

In my first year of law I almost literally starved to death; most young lawyers do. When there was nothing to do in those days it was my habit to visit the offices of a young lawyer friend of mine who, thanks to a man who came into his office each Saturday to change his will, was making a few bucks. One day I arrived while he was reading his mail. The mail included an invitation from the city's Businessmen's Association to enter a float in an upcoming parade; the letter had been sent to all businessmen in town and lawyers, of course, are businessmen. We spent a long time that day discussing the pipe dream of a lawyer's float in a parade. Our final picture was that of me robed as a judge, listening to my friend as he read from a law book. One of our wives would stand, dressed in white and blindfolded, at the front of the float, carrying the scales of justice. Our children, begarbed in colorful wear, would throw our business cards to people along the parade route. Our names, of course, would be emblazoned in colorful flowers on the side of the float. It was just a dream—that float would have got us both disbarred the next day. Our one day of glory would be paid for by never practicing law again. We laughed about it, of course, and opined that a lawyer's float could never be. Like all lawyers of that era, however, we could not foresee the deluge of young lawyers in the 1970s and the resultant opening of the ad door. In 1985 you will be seeing many a parade float like the one here described. I hope I am around to see them, though I'm not sure I'll believe what I see.

Even today, when lawyer advertising is in its early days, most writers on the subject feel that the listing of specializations will be as far as lawyers will ever be permitted to go. They are of the same breed as the men who proclaimed in 1912 that two percent was about as far as federal income tax would go. In almost every instance, in tracking the background of these writers, I have found that they are in the upper (richer) echelons of law practice. They do not know of the comparative ghetto existence of just-out-of-law-school lawyers, or of older lawyers who have never made it to the top. While these older lawyers are not strictly of the "ghetto," they are certainly poorly off by comparison with those many lawyers who are earning $100,000 a year and more. The "ghetto" lawyers want to make it to the top with their rich brethren, and they see advertising as the means of achieving this end.

A conservative ad of the near-future may feature a flashing neon sign in letters two feet high announcing, say, HARVEY MILLTOWN, LAWYER, while a neon arrow points down towards his office door. Other lawyers will run daily ads in the local newspaper announcing, for example:

GLADYS AWRIGHT,
Attorney-at-Law
A competent attorney to suit your every need.
(Address and phone numbers listed)

The majority, however, will seek to outdo each other. Try it for yourself. As you watch ads on TV today, imagine that the product being sold is a lawyer and his services. With a subtle change here and there the lawyer will be advertised in a way appealing to most viewers, e.g., "Don't squeeze the Charmin or I'll call Attorney Isaac Witherbothom to file suit against you."

"Need a lawsuit? Attorney Billy Bottom's two-for-one sale will be going on all this week at 3344 Adirondack Avenue, Tweedlesville. If you only have one lawsuit come in anyway. Billy is a specialist at finding other lawsuits people might have. See Billy today and sue tomorrow."

"It's not nice to fool Mother Law. Only Wiltse Will-win, our town's leading attorney, can help you out of the trouble you'll be in when you start fooling around with the law."

"If you think dining at the Waldorf Astoria is perfection, then you've missed the buffet served daily at the offices of Attorney Ima Groaner. Clients, both new and old, are welcome to partake of these delicacies between noon and 2:00 P.M., Sundays excluded. Cost of dining included in fees."

"ENJOY THE 'HAPPY HOUR' WITH LAWYER LARRY LURKING! Between 5 and 7 P.M. drinks of all kinds are available for only 24¢ in the Lurking Law Offices at 12345 Gotcha Street. Lurking, specializing in drunk driving cases, joins guests for free bar-side consultations during this period."

"In fee tests run by the Consumers Fee Guide of America, it was found that Attorney G. Q. Mileage outstripped all competitors. The mileage you get from his fees is the greatest, his fees the lowest of 2,000 attorneys tested at random. See or call him today at [address, phone numbers]."

"Bothered by aching back, aching feet, sore body muscles? You probably have a lawsuit to file against someone. It's both fashionable and money prudent to be suing someone today. Time, then, that you contacted Attorney Werner Barratray to start your suit. If you don't know exactly who it is you should sue, Werner will find that person, or hopefully that corporation, for you.''

Spot ads on TV or radio, and more than likely in the newspapers, might include these:

DOES YOUR HUSBAND RUN AROUND WITH OTHER WOMEN OR DRINK TOO MUCH? IF SO, HE'S SPENDING MONEY THAT HE SHOULD BE SPENDING ON YOU. YOUR FRUSTRATIONS AND WEARINESS CAN BE CURED BY FILING FOR DIVORCE TODAY WITH *J. Paul Getme*, [address and phone].

IN TROUBLE WITH THE LAW? SEE A MAN WHO KNOWS THE COPS AND IS A FRIEND OF ALL JUDGES. IF A DEAL CAN BE MADE HE'LL MAKE IT—*Worthington Worthwhile*, THE FABULOUS CRIMINAL ATTORNEY WITH OFFICES AT [address]. CALL HIM DAY OR NIGHT AT [phone number].

DID YOUR DOCTOR REALLY CURE YOU? ARE YOU HAPPY WITH THE WAY YOUR FORMER LAWYER HANDLED YOUR LAST CASE? IF YOUR ANSWERS TO THESE QUESTIONS ARE ''NO'' YOU PROBABLY HAVE AN EXCELLENT SUIT FOR MALPRACTICE. SUE NOW, PAY LATER, WITH ATTORNEY *William Suemall*, A SPECIALIST EXTRAORDINAIRE IN MALPRACTICE ACTIONS. [Address and phone number].

TIRED OF PAYING INCOME TAX? IF YOU ARE THEN JUST DON'T PAY IT THIS YEAR. WHEN THE GOVERNMENT SUES YOU FOR THE TAXES CONTACT ATTORNEYS *Weir, Eggsbert and Champions* [address] FOR YOUR DEFENSE. WE GUARANTEE TO SETTLE WITH THE GOVERNMENT AT 50¢ ON THE DOLLAR. OUR FEE? ONE-HALF OF WHAT YOU SAVE, LEAVING YOU WITH ONE-QUARTER LESS THAN YOU WOULD HAVE PAID HAD YOU BEEN FOOLISH ENOUGH TO PAY YOUR TAX THIS YEAR!

BACK FROM YOUR HONEYMOON? THINGS NOT GOING THE WAY YOU EXPECTED? HUSBAND "CHANGED" FROM THE WAY HE WAS DURING YOUR COURTING DAYS? See *Karl Annulitt* TODAY FOR ANNULMENT OF YOUR MARRIAGE. "LOW FEE" KARL CAN BE REACHED AT (phone number) OR VISIT HIS OFFICES AT [address].

Billboards and signs now seen in front of stores may read (following the lawyer's name and address):

FIFTY PERCENT OFF ON ALL DIVORCES THIS WEEK ONLY. TODAY'S SPECIAL: SIMPLE WILLS $10, FREE WITH EACH NEW DIVORCE.

LOWEST FEES IN TOWN FOR MALPRACTICE CASES. SHOP AROUND AND THEN SEE US. WE'LL BEAT ANY FEE-CHARGE OUR COMPETITION MAY OFFER YOU.

TODAY'S SPECIAL: Divorces, 25% off; Wills, $5.00; Personal Injury Suits, 10% of your recovery (the lowest fee in town!).

WANTED: LAWSUITS AGAINST YOUR NEIGHBORS. FEE ZERO. NEED SUCH CASES TO ESTABLISH LEGAL PRECEDENT FOR NEIGHBORHOOD CASES NOW ON APPEAL. ("Costs deposit" required.)

TRADE YOUR OLD LAWYER IN FOR HARVEY MILLSTONE. HE'S THE BEST AND *YOU* DESERVE HIM!

DO YOU DREAM OF FARAWAY PLACES WITH STRANGE SOUNDING NAMES? WANT TO GO BUT DON'T HAVE THE MONEY? SEE ME TODAY. CHANCES ARE YOU HAVE A LAWSUIT THAT WILL GET YOU THE MONEY YOU NEED. WE'LL SUE FOR YOU!

SUITS AGAINST DOCTORS AND CORPORATIONS A SPECIALITY. LIST OF SATISFIED CUSTOMERS AVAILABLE. SUE NOW!

LAWSUITS CAN BE FUN WITH *Suem & Sigh*. LIVE IT UP
THROUGH LAWSUITS. WALK AWAY A WINNER EVERY
TIME!

DIVORCES ARE FUNSVILLE! FREE COMPUTER DATING
SERVICE AVAILABLE WHILE YOUR CASE IS PENDING.
ATTORNEY MEMBER SCREEN ACTOR'S GUILD.

Examples of such ads are commonplace. An excellent example involves a judge who, a few years ago, was handling the traffic ticket cases in his particular courthouse. If the defendant was a comely young woman the judge would see her in his chambers. There he would outline this proposition for her: advise her he would fine her X number of dollars (usually a large amount) *or* she could spend a night with him in a motel—only a couple of hours if she were married—and the fine would be forgotten. All went well for him until one young lady blew the proverbial whistle. The bar association stepped in, followed by the Judicial Council (the group that keeps judges in line). A few days before he was scheduled to be thrown off the bench, and in the midst of daily newspaper stories about the case, he resigned and went back to practicing law. Lawyers practicing in his area told me that after that women clients flocked to his offices for any kind of case they could dream up. The newspapers had given him plenty of free "advertising" and apparently many women liked the product he was dispensing.

An executive of the Newspaper Advertising Bureau recently estimated that lawyers could spend a quarter of a million dollars a year for ads. The estimate is extremely low. Madison Avenue advertising firms, expecting large incomes from lawyer advertising, will find their dreams a bit tarnished when it becomes evident that the vast majority of lawyers are ingenious enough to do their own ad work. Only the larger, more prestigious law firms, finally bowing to the trend of the times, will take their accounts to the big ad houses.

The bulk of lawyer advertising, unfortunately, will

be by young and inexperienced lawyers, shysters, poor lawyers who think it's time they became rich, but only here and there by good lawyers who are suddenly losing business and need to fight back. Herein lies the clue to beating this "game" when it is thrust upon the lay public.

What can you do about it?

1. The chief suggestion would be to avoid those lawyers who advertise in gaudy and hucksterlike fashion. They will be the inexperienced or shyster lawyers. Using the method repeated so often, choose instead a lawyer recommended by the bar or by friends or who only advertises a bar association *approved* specialty. By the 1980s most bar associations should have classified specialty lists of attorneys who meet grueling bar standards. The practice of law is becoming highly specialized and the day of the general practicioner will soon be over. Seeking the specialist betters your chances of obtaining a successful conclusion to your legal action.

2. In going through the yellow pages of the future, select a lawyer who legitimately specializes in the field of your case. Do not choose one who merely claims he specializes in certain fields; choose one whom the bar has sanctioned. An entry in your local directory might read:

> SILVERMAN, Ronald O.
> Certified Specialist in:
>   (1) Workmen's Compensation Law
>   (2) General Personal Injury Law
> Approved by the Board of Legal
>   Specialization of (your state)
> (address and phone number)

If your case falls within the fields in which Mr. Silverman specializes you would know that he has met the rigid qualifications which your state's bar association had set up for specialists in those fields.

3. The coming advertising boom will hurt the happy-client referral system but it will always remain your best bet in the selection of a good attorney.

4. Beware the attorney who blows his own horn. The garish advertisers belong on Madison Avenue, not in a courtroom.

CHAPTER 10

Advertising Update

Books are not written in a day nor published in a week. *Gone With the Wind*, written in the early 1920s, didn't see the light of day until 1936. Nine publishers had turned it down and the tenth, who finally took a chance on it, found it mouldering in the author's Atlanta attic. Alex Haley took twelve years to pen *Roots*.

Nor was this book written in a day. Unlike Haley, however, I was pressed for time because the subject matter was topical, concerned with what lawyers are doing *today*, not what they might have been doing during the Civil War. During my writing, a case (that bore tremendously on the subject of lawyers' advertising) was awaiting a hearing in the United States Supreme Court. There was one probable outcome to the case; two possibles lurked in the background. As the probable outcome would not significantly change lawyer advertising in 1977 there seemed no need to discuss it. It was one of the "possibles" that finally came to pass when the highest court in the country handed down its decision on June 27, 1977. The door to full-scale advertising, as discussed in the previous chapter, now seemed to open wide. The probability that the Supreme Court would uphold state bar associations' nationwide bans on advertising or, at most, allow advertising to a limited degree, was left at the starting gate. The right to advertise won the race.

Bates, et al v. State Bar of Arizona started, as do many cases, with a person or group of persons challenging the law. In this particular matter the law was Arizona's ban on advertising by lawyers. The challengers were two young Arizona lawyers, Bates and O'Steen, who had opened a legal clinic and advertised the fact in the paper. They went further. To

117

the shock of the Arizona State Bar these young lawyers advertised that they were offering "legal services
at very reasonable fees." They went so far as to list
their exact fees for uncontested divorces and adoptions, simple bankruptcies and changes-of-name
proceedings. The State Bar, in high dudgeon, filed suit
to restrain them from this nefarious activity.

The trial court, as might be expected, upheld the
State Bar. Appealing, the advertising lawyers were
again thwarted at the Arizona Supreme Court level.
That august body threw the case out, refusing to accept the advertising-lawyers' claim that the advertising ban rule violated the federal Sherman Act because
it tended to limit competition; the court likewise found
that the ad ban did not infringe on the appellants'
rights under the First Amendment of the United States
Constitution.

Fighting for the right to tell the world they'd handle
uncontested divorces for $175 and bankruptcies for
$250, the two Phoenix lawyer-appellants, trudged on
the United States Supreme Court. It may sometimes
take a year for that supreme body to announce a decision. The Bates appeal, for example, was filed with the
court in 1976, argued in open court on January 18 of
1977 and the court's decision was released more than
five months later.

Few lawyers would have wagered that the high
court's decision would deliver such a staggering blow
to the nationwide ban on advertising by lawyers. My
own thoughts were pleasant ones for the predictions of
my previous chapter had now come to pass (albeit a
few years earlier than I had expected). The reader can
judge for himself as he reads the summary of Justice
Blackmun's opinion of the court:

1. [Throws out appellants' arguments that the ad
   ban violated their rights under the Sherman Act.]
2. Commercial Speech, which serves individual
   and social interests in assuring informed and reliable decision-making, is entitled to some First

Amendment protection . . . and the justifications advanced by the appellee [Arizona State Bar] are inadequate to support the suppression of all advertising by lawyers.

(a) This case does not involve any question concerning in-person solicitation or advertising as to the *quality* of legal service, but only the question whether lawyers may constitutionally advertise the *prices* at which routine services will be performed.

(b) The belief that lawyers are somehow above "trade" is an anachronism, and for a lawyer to advertise his fees will not undermine true professionalism.

(c) *Advertising legal services is not inherently misleading.* [Emphasis mine] Only routine services lend themselves to advertising and for such services fixed rates can be meaningfully established. . . . Although a client may not know the detail involved in a given task he can identify the service at the level of generality to which advertising lends itself. Though advertising does not provide a complete foundation on which to select an attorney, it would be peculiar to deny the consumer at least some of the relevant information needed for an informed decision on the ground that the information was not complete.

(d) Advertising, the traditional mechanism in a free-market economy for supplier to inform potential purchaser of the availability of terms of exchange, may well benefit the administration of justice.

(e) It is entirely possible that advertising will serve to reduce, not advance, the cost of legal services to the consumer and may well aid new attorneys in entering the market.

(f) An attorney who is inclined to cut quality will do so regardless of the rule on advertising, the restraints on which are an ineffective deterrent to shoddy work.

(g) Undue enforcement problems need not be anticipated, and *it is at least incongruous for the opponents of advertising to extol the virtues of the legal profession while also asserting that through advertising lawyers will mislead their clients.* [Emphasis mine. Attention is called to my remarks in chapter 1 to the effect that lawyers' associations have, for centuries, been trying to whitewash the entire profession, never admitting that a few "bad guys" exist in their ranks.]

3. [Throws out a minor argument presented by the appellant lawyers that does not affect the overall decision.]

4. On this record, appellants' advertisement (contrary to appellee's contention) is not misleading and falls within the scope of First Amendment protection.

(a) The term 'legal clinic' would not be understood to refer to an operation like appellants' that is geared to provide standardized and multiple services.

(b) The advertisement's claim that appellants offer services at "very reasonable" prices is not misleading. Appellants' advertised fee for an uncontested divorce, which was specifically cited by appellee, is in line with customary charges in the area.

(c) Appellants' failure to disclose that a name change might be accomplished by the client without an attorney's aid was not misleading since the difficulty of performing the task is not revealed and since most legal services may be performed legally by the citizen himself.

Guidelines for the future—perhaps the vital crux of the opinion—were found in Justice Blackmun's advice that "Advertising that is false, deceptive or misleading of course is subject to restraint. . . . It follows as well that there may be reasonable restrictions on the time, place and manner of advertising."

The true significance of the decision lies in the words "false, deceptive or misleading." Advertising along these lines has always been banned. Until now it has applied to the butcher, baker, candlestick maker, car dealer, food-market operator and the wide, wide world of commodity selling as well as most services. Today it applies to legal services as well. The doors have opened.

The clause in the decision that state bar associations have clasped to their breasts is the one which says they may place "reasonable restrictions on the time, place and manner of advertising." What does this *mean*? It sounds simple enough but is so general it could mean anything. State bar associations everywhere are trying to evaluate the situation so that they can reword their Rules of Ethics regarding advertising. They will, of course, be bound by *Bates v. State Bar of Arizona*. Most, at the outset, will come out with stop-gap opinions such as Lily Barry, Chief Disciplinary Counsel for the California Bar made for that state's lawyers soon after the Bates decision.

"The position we've taken," Ms. Barry stated, "is that whatever is done under Bates [v. Arizona State Bar] as narrowly construed, is not actionable. *Deviations from the ruling would be done at the attorney's own risk.*" [Emphasis mine.]

Two of a still small number of ads which attorneys have placed since Ms. Barry's opinion read as follows:

LAW OFFICES
Victor Beaglehofer
Special emphasis on Personal
Injury & Insurance problems.
Will quote fees for other legal
Services.

The Gotobed ad conforms to the letter with the high
court's decision in Bates. Is the Beaglehofer ad a
"deviation" from the Bates ruling? It quotes no
prices, but says Beaglehofer will quote fees. Certainly
it is not false, deceptive or misleading. Yet it takes a
small step forward for legal advertising in that it does
not hew exactly to the wording of the ad which the
Bates Clinic placed, and which was the only ad before
the Supreme Court in their historic advertising decision. Will the State Bar come down on Mr. Beaglehofer because, for some reason, his ad was not done in
the proper "manner" (to quote the court) and was a
"deviation" (to quote Ms. Barry) from the Bates ad?
The Beaglehofer ad, like Gotobed's, is certainly
dignified and to the point. Will that satisfy the state
bar?

No one knows as yet. What is known is that the
state bar's board of governors has submitted a plan for
limited attorney advertising. What does "limited"
mean? No one knows as yet. Every state bar is
presently formulating such plans and you can bet your
bottom dollar all of them will allow *limited* advertising.

While you're in a betting mood parlay this bet to one
that wagers that within a few days after California's—or any state's—new advertising rules are
published, some lawyer will produce a far-out ad that
will fly directly in the teeth of the limitations his bar
association will place on "the time, place and manner" of advertising. That state bar will then sue to en-
join his ad and, by 1980, his suits and countless other
such actions, will reach the United States Supreme
Court again. If these ads do not falsely or deceptively
mislead the public it may be comfortably predicted

that the high court will uphold the advertising lawyers. The Pandora's box of advertising will then be open and ads as viewed in the previous chapter will be commonplace.

Find an ad in the previous chapter that is "false and misleading." Many are garish and some tread that tightrope wire of "sales talk." The latter is best defined as the giving of the seller's own opinion of the goods or services he has to offer. He warrants nothing. Sales talk has been given much legal leeway in the business world and lawyers will profit from it. By 1980 the ads we see will be far from "dignified" in the bar association concept of the word. But the lawyer then will be more interested in making a buck than in being dignified.

The bans which bar associations have placed on advertising relate closely to the "reserve clause" which professional sports have long used to control the signing up and retaining of players. The "ownership" of human bodies, which still prevails to a great extent in the world of professional sports, has always been completely unconstitutional. The owners have always known it. They know too, however, that unless this clause is kept in effect the players will flock to the clubs which offer the most money or which are located in salubrious spots (it's more fun playing football on a balmy day in Los Angeles than in a Buffalo snowstorm). And they are right. The recent inroads being made into the reserve clause are having their effect.

"I'm not going to play football next year unless my team trades me to a team on the West Coast," pouts a star playing on a money-plagued midwestern team.

My! it can get cold in Green Bay if you were born and raised in Miami Beach!

The current flock of "free agents" are going where the money is. They will continue to do so. Owners know that professional sports as we know them are doomed. But, for the most part, they are older men and will not be around by the close of the century when the present-day football, basketball and baseball leagues will have disappeared. Their early counterparts predicted an incurable cancer in sports should teams lose control of their players. They were right. Though they still look good on paper, pro sports are dying.

Bar associations have always known, too, that if lawyers were allowed to advertise, the associations would eventually lose control of their members. As professional ball teams would eventually die if their players were given complete freedom (of which the ''free agent system'' is the next-to-last step), so would the disciplinary powers of bar associations once fulltilt advertising was allowed. Contrary to widespread opinion, bar associations are set up in great part to protect the public from unethical lawyers. They valiantly try to winnow out the bad guys so that you, the potential client, will not be stuck with the games-playing shyster. They are losing the battle because their comparatively small staffs cannot cope with the tremendous influx of new lawyers. They lose more ground now that they cannot control what lawyers advertise about themselves. In no lawyer ads that you read today, or that you read years hence, will a lawyer ever say:

(a) I am a brand-new lawyer and you will be my first case, or

(b) I am an old lawyer with much experience but I booze it up far more than I should, or

(c) I am a fine lawyer *but* am in desperate need of money for alimony, child support and the upkeep of my mistress, my Cadillac and the local racetrack; *you*, by heeding the siren song of this ad, will provide me with that money.

You won't see ads like that. These things are for you to find out once you've followed the ad to the lawyer's ''store.''

A lawyer's ad will be no different from grocery store ads. Of the 2,000 items they have to sell, the latter advertise only a dozen or so. These ''loss leaders'' are designed to draw you into the store. Once there you'll undoubtedly do the rest of your weekly shopping. The prices you pay for other items may be higher than at a market down the street but few people, once grabbed, buy only the loss leaders and go on to the next store for their underpriced goodies.

The advertising lawyer wants you in his office. Once there, either ethically or through playing some of the games enumerated in this book, he will keep you. Once there you will find the $150 "simple divorce" does not apply to the facts of your case. You will end up paying more. All lawyers know that clients are inclined to oversimplify their cases. Few realize the welter of laws, rules, forms, documents, affidavits and court decisions that convert the path of even the simplest case into an obstacle course. Through the use of the "good-case, bad-case" technique the money-hungry attorney can make the client part with a few more dollars than was advertised. But this is not the attorney's fault. It is the fault of the system under which he operates. Once captured, the client can only pray that he has an ethical lawyer. The chances of his prayers being answered, however, are lessening every year.

Justice Blackmun, in *Bates v. Arizona,* said that an attorney who does less than quality work will do so regardless of the ban on advertising. The ad ban, he felt, would *not* be an effective deterrent to shoddy work. What the entire court failed to realize, however, was that the number of shoddy lawyers did not include the small handful that were around when the justices were young lawyers. They failed to realize that the number of unethical lawyers has increased to near-epidemic proportions. Significantly, and sadly, they have, through the Bates case, allowed the bad guys to advertise themselves as the good guys. The bar association, standing by as the sheriff, is powerless to stop the jailbreak. How does the public know that HENRY WUNNERFUL, a lawyer handling all types of cases at modest fees, is the most unethical lawyer in town? How too will they know that

ROBERT JACKSON JOHNSON
Attorney-at-law
Personal Injury Case Specialist

is the best attorney in the state in his field and that economics forced him to advertise?

No, the ban on advertising never affected the ethical lawyer. He wouldn't have advertised anyway. Through reputation, civic work and politics he'd have made his way without the ballyhoo. It has always been the lesser lawyer pushing for the complete abolishment of the ban on advertising and he is the one, through Bates and its follow-up cases, who will win the battle.

Bates and his partner are probably fine young lawyers. Their ad was modest in comparison to the ads-of-the-future discussed in the previous chapter. Several very able young lawyers of my own acquaintance have placed neat little ads in the classified section of our local paper. Through their abilities they will eventually make the grade in the legal world; through small ads they only hope to speed up the process. A goodly number of ethical lawyers will advertise but the majority of the advertisers will be the free-wheelers who are out to play games with your money.

What you can do about the advertising game

1. The advice given at the close of the previous chapter on advertising will still stand you in good stead. Those points are even more important to you today than when that chapter was first written. The Bates case was still sleeping quietly at that time.

2. If you must select an attorney through ads, select one whose song is soft and low-key. The probabilities are that the wilder the ad, the worse the attorney who lies behind it. Good attorneys, whether younger ones seeking to get established or older ones pressed by the loss of business to the dazzling-ad shy-

sters, will always come on in quiet dignity. Law is a serious business. It is not the razzle-dazzle, thrill-a-minute game that television would have you believe it is. Nor is it, in the main, as simple a proposition as many ads will lead you to believe.

3. Selection of an attorney through state or local bar association lists will become increasingly important to you now that the lid has been taken off the advertising can. Stung by such a wholesale abolishment of advertising as occurred in *Bates v. Arizona*, bar associations will be quick to file further suits to stop such ads as defy new, post-Bates, state rules on advertising.

Until the Supreme Court says otherwise these new state rules will prevail. It is hoped that if, in defiance of state bar rules, a lawyer should advertise in a verboten manner, his name will be stricken from the list of lawyers recommended by your association. If bar associations will have the guts to do this—at least until the U.S. Supreme Court okays full-tilt advertising—you will, for a few more years at least, be better assured of getting the name of an ethical lawyer from your own association.

4. Never forget that in legal work, as in any other kind of business, you always get what you pay for. Will your $49 uncontested divorce through Lawyer A bring the same results as had you gone to Lawyer B? The latter was charging the prevailing rate in town (as witnessed through ads) of $195. Will a $1.98 fishing pole serve you as well as a $50.00 Daiwa? Would the Mudville semi-pro Mudcats beat the 1977 Dodgers in a best-of-seven baseball series?

You know the answers. I believe the American public is smarter than the shyster thinks it is. Let's hope I'm right.

This is the advertisement heard "round the world." Modest in its lay-out, it little suspected that it would go to the Supreme Court of the United States and make legal history:

*From the *American Bar Association Journal, vol. 63*, March 1977, p. 344.*

CHAPTER 11

Wills and Probate

Wills are something every lawyer likes to draw. He amasses them in his early and middle years. He is then sustained in his old age by probating the wills he drew in those earlier years. The trick, of course, is to outlive the client. An 80-year-old lawyer drawing a will for a 25-year-old man has little chance of probating *that* will; turn the figures around, however, and within a few years that now 30-year-old lawyer will be probating his first will.

The games lawyers play in the writing of wills are rather difficult to perceive and, more likely than not, the client will never know a game is involved. Example: an aging tightwad, worth a million and hoping somehow he can take it with him, visits a young lawyer for a will. The lawyer has never probated a will and perhaps never drafted one. Perceiving the fees to come from probating such a large estate, however, he agrees to draw the will for nothing. The old man, always liking a bargain, is thrilled. The will is drawn. The trouble with the "draw a will for nothing" game is that established and reputable lawyers will often play it too. Finding a million-dollar estate is a rarity and so charging little or nothing to draw a will for a person holding such an estate is commonplace, but there is really no way of knowing what you are getting when no fee is charged.

"No fees" can backfire. I learned this from a lawyer while going to law school. He was in law school too. An old-timer from West Texas, he had been admitted to practice in the days when it was possible to study in an attorney's office for a period of years, then take the bar exams and become a lawyer. Having served in World War II, thanks to the G.I. Bill, he could afford to take three years off to go to law school. During our wills class he discussed the problem of what to charge for wills—somewhere between "nothing" and "too much" was the answer.

"I recall," he said, "writing wills for nothing. Then, when the person died, his executor would go to some other lawyer because they figured I was pretty cheap to charge zero. When I started charging for wills I would sometimes find the executor going elsewhere on the theory that since I overcharged for the will I would overcharge for probating the estate. You really can't win all the time in the wills fee game."

Getting you to name the lawyer as executor of your estate is another game often played. In many states a lawyer can be both lawyer and executor for an estate. In such cases he might well get a double fee for little extra work. Where he can be only one or the other, he will choose to be executor because his fee in most cases will be the same as the attorney's. If not, the attorney can give him a referral fee to bring his "jack" as executor up to a higher level. Since the executor chooses the attorney in most instances, the executor/attorney will refer the attorney portion of the estate over to an attorney friend. If a friend or relative is named as executor he often, after the client's demise, takes the will for probate to his own attorney. Thus it is that attorneys strive to have themselves named as executor in many instances. Play the game as you see it, though. While experienced probate attorneys are good executors, how are you to know that this lawyer is an "experienced probate attorney?" Trust departments of banks make the best executors because they are in the business, primarily, of being executors. If the attorney suggests this route you can be sure he knows what he's doing.

Probate of a will occurs after the death of the person for whom it was drawn. Probate laws are cumbersome in every state. Though never now as long and drawn-out as the Jarndyce Estate in Dicken's *Bleak House*, they do consume more time, often years, than would appear necessary. Reform is underway and young people today can look forward to speedy probating of their estates when, fifty years from now, they cross the River Styx. This thought should make them rest more comfortably when the time comes!

We are, however, speaking of today. What games will lawyers play in probate cases in this era?

The fee game is the principal game the lawyer plays in probate, for in almost every instance it was the probate fee to be involved that led him to draw the will for little or no cost at the outset. In our country there is no standard probate fee. States divide into three classes insofar as fees are concerned:

(a) where the law sets no fee and the lawyer can get as much as he is able,

(b) where a flat fee (e.g., 10 percent) is charged on the value of an estate, no matter how big or small, and

(c) where a percentage fee graduates downwards as the size of an estate goes upwards. California has the latter system; law there provides for a fee of 7 percent of the first $1,000 value of an estate, 4 percent of the next $9,000, 3 percent of the next $40,000, 2 percent of the next $100,000, 1½ percent of the next $350,000 and 1 percent of that part of the gross estate over $500,000. In an estate of $100,000 in a flat fee (using 10 percent as the example) state, the attorney's fee would be $10,000; in California the fee would be $2,630. Probate attorneys in California advise that they make their money by probating wills on a volume basis. They generally feel that they put $1,500 worth of time into the average estate and since the average case produces a fee well below $1,500, they can make money only by appearing in court on "probate days" with several wills to probate. As it is for the average personal injury attorney, the million-dollar probate is a rare bonanza for the probate lawyer.

In states with a graduated percentage allowed for fees, attorneys play at a game known as "extraordinary fees." Such fees are paid to the lawyer for work over and above the exact legal work he is called upon to perform in the probate. California, by statutory law, sets up a number of items that are considered as "extraordinary." These include:

(a) securing loans or assisting in sales of the decedent's property

(b) contesting or litigating claims for or against the estate

(c) preparation of tax returns (in lieu of an accountant)

(d) adjustment, or litigation or payment of any taxes

(e) litigation—suing or defending—regarding property in the estate

(f) carrying on the business of the decedent while the estate is pending, and

(g) (the "catchall") "such other litigation or special services as the representative may have to prosecute, defend or perform."*

In the majority of probates, where extraordinary fees are allowed by law, such fees are requested. Sometimes the judge turns down the requests and often will give the fee but lower the amount requested by the lawyer. My early sorrow for lawyers in California getting such small percentage fees (after I'd come from Texas where, at the time, your fee was anything you could get!) was soon displaced by envy when I found out about "extraordinary fees." From a game point of view, most of the extra work performed by the lawyer is justified, but just enough work is not justified to make it a game the public should be wary of. Could an accountant perform the tax work for less? Could the executor run the business at no cost to the estate (e.g., if the executor is the heir who will get the decedent's place of business when probate is finished)? Could a claim against the estate be settled amicably rather than tried as a lawsuit against the es-

---

*Arthur K. Marshall, Superior Court Judge, *California Probate Handbook*, 2d ed. (Parker & Sons Publications, Inc., 1963), pp. 149–52.

tate (trying a case brings a higher fee than early settlement does!)?

The "anything you can get" fee sounds like Heaven for lawyers but it can boomerang to the client's advantage. Not too many years ago, traveling through West Texas, I stopped off to see an old law school friend of mine named Shelby. He told me the following story to illustrate the adverse effect the "no set fee" probate might have on attorneys:

An elderly gentleman had died in a town nearby. He left no will so his widow and sole heir would become the administratrix of his estate. His estate was considerable. There were four lawyers in the county. My friend, like the other three, was eager to handle the estate but, being an ethical lawyer, did not go a-courtin' the widow. Eventually she visited the office of my friend. I don't recall the exact figures now but when she asked him what his fee would be, he said $10,000. She then informed him she'd seen Lawyer A (one of the county's four) and he'd set $9,000 as his fee. Shelby said he'd go $8,750. She left to think it over. He knew, as proved true, that she'd visit lawyers C and D in their respective towns as her next order of business. When, a week later, she got back to Shelby, the fee was down to $5,000—a figure quoted by A when he learned D's price was $5,500.

Would Shelby take it for less than $5,000? That was the question he was pondering when I rolled through town. By now, he explained, the widow was getting down to the bare bones in seeking. If all went well he wouldn't lose money at $4,500 but he wouldn't make much either. If matters went awry somewhere along the way, as often happens in probates, the case could be a disaster. All of his time might be wrapped up in this one case and he would have to turn down other business. If, for example, he was earning $15,000 a year and the time he spent on the widow's case dragged his income down to, say, $7,000 for the next year, he could be wiped out. When I left town the next morning he was still deciding what to tell the widow when she came to see him later in the day. My guess is that Lawyer A got the case, and regretted it!

In "flat fee" states the law still may allow the "extraordinary fees" game, although, if the set fee be 10 percent, the extra things the lawyer might do for money would be much more limited than is the case in California. In these states, as in the graduated percentage states, the attorney who is long on gall and short on ethics might ask you for "money on the side" to handle your case because the estate is so small and his work will be so tremendous by comparison. Don't do it. Taking money on the side, or under the table, is contrary to the Code of Ethics and an attorney practicing this custom is not to be trusted!

What you can do about probate games

1. At the very outset of the probate, on your first visit to a lawyer's office to retain him to probate the estate in which you are heir or executor, determine the attorney fee allowed by law in your state. Then ask about "extraordinary fees." If he says there will be none, get it in writing! Should he be frank and outline the extraordinary work he expects might be performed, inquire of him as to each item that is not clear to you. What fee will he ask for doing this or that? Could it be done more cheaply elsewhere? Is it necessary at all?

2. Claims against an estate drain money from that estate if each one is battled out in a separate lawsuit. Be settlement-minded on every claim. Would it be cheaper to pay the claim than it would be to litigate it? Trying the case will bring the *lawyer* more money. Will his increase in fees overshadow whatever the lawsuit gained by being tried? Go into each claim thoroughly with your attorney. Weigh your chances of winning or losing the suit, independently of his advice, before you reach a decision.

3. If, when asking for fees at probate's end, the attorney requests higher extraordinary fees than you feel he is entitled to, be at the hearing and tell it to the judge—either in person if law allows, or through another attorney. After all, if you're an executor/heir it's *your* money he's talking about spending.

4. If you find out that your state's probate fees are "whatever the attorney can get," then shop around a bit as the West Texas widow did. Chances are you'll come out of it with a more than reasonable fee (from your point of view!) being charged. Let each lawyer know what the attorney you saw before him quoted feewise.

5. If your area lists specializations for lawyers choose only those listed as "probate specialists." If not so listed, check with your bar association. Failing there, the "friends and relatives route" is again recommended. Seeing an attorney "cold" is taking a chance. The odds of finding a reliable attorney favor you today but tomorrow, in the grand and glorious era of anything-goes advertising, who knows?

6. Both probate lawyers and the public will benefit from limited advertising now available through the Yellow Pages. Though flagrant, far-out advertising will hurt the consumer and weaken Law as a profession, probate attorneys will now be able to insert notice of their specialties in the phone books; should state bar associations certify them as specialists in this field, this fact will also be noted. The prospective client, noting that a lawyer is a state bar certified specialist, will be doubly protected. Until now the mass of attorney names in the Yellow Pages has given no indication as to which few of the many are dyed-in-the-wool probate specialists. Advertising, on a limited scale, will have some benefits!

7. Beware the far-out advertising attorney who claims to be a probate specialist or who lists "probate" among a dozen specialties he practices. The probate attorney generally does little else. Unlike his flamboyant, out-going brethren, the trial attorneys,

he is a quiet, low-key individual not given to histrionics, much less garish advertising. He will be the last to advertise and, when he does, will only place the limited ad noting his specialty.

CHAPTER 12

The "What Is Your Fee?" Game

In 1872 the Sedgwick County, Kansas, Bar Association set up a Minimum Fee Schedule for lawyers to follow in the setting of their fees. It was suggested that, while lawyers could charge as much as they wanted, they should keep their minimum fees in line with the schedule the Bar Association had published. By the 1970s the number of local bar associations publishing minimum fee schedules had risen to nearly 1,000 across the nation; few states were without such guidelines.

Although it was never quite established why a "minimum" fee was this much or that much for the wide variety of services* set forth in these schedules, it was generally assumed that the fees were those that a young lawyer with a practice fairly well established after, say, four or five years, should be charging. While older lawyers could and did, because of their experience, charge more, and while specialists in a particular field could charge more because of their expertise, charging fees below the minimum fee schedule was looked on as "fee cutting." While such practice was not considered unethical, bar associations frowned on it. Lawyers, they felt, were not competing in a market place at cut-rate prices but were offering valuable services that should be paid for at par.

Such fee schedules came in handy for most lawyers. Often there could be a lapse of several years or more

---

*The 1968 Long Beach, California ADVISORY MINIMUM FEE SCHEDULE (note use of the word "advisory") contained twenty-one varieties of legal work with many subheadings under each of them, e.g., ADOPTION: (a) Consent, (b) Abandonment additional, (c) Agency, (d) Step parent, (e) Sole Custody and (f) Contested adoption (per day, additional.)

between cases of certain types. A man might handle an adoption once every ten years or a bankruptcy once every five. The fee schedule was a useful tool for determining what fees were being currently charged for such services. A glance, in 1972, at the 1948 fee schedules found legal fees advancing very little when compared to the nation's overall cost of living increase. In many instances clients unhappy with a quoted fee were shown the minimum fee schedule as proof that this was the least the lawyer could charge—that elsewhere in town the client might be charged much more. They served a good purpose and saved the public from cut-rate lawyers who invariably did cut-rate work. You get what you pay for.

Ralph Nader, however, looked on minimum fee schedules as price fixing. In his opinion such schedules were unlawful. Lawyers ought to have the right to cut prices and compete in the market place by offering bargains. Competition, he opined, would make the field of law healthier. His chance to attack such schedules came along in the person of Louis Goldfarb who was himself an attorney. Goldfarb and his wife were purchasing a home in Virginia. In that state a procedure known as a Title Search was required before title insurance could be secured and title insurance was, in turn, required before a home could be purchased. One attorney quoted him a fee of $522.50 for such a search (the home in question was priced at $54,000 in a rising market). This attorney told the Goldfarbs that $522.50 was the *minimum* fee allowed under Virginia fee schedules. The Goldfarbs contacted dozens of lawyers, but $522.50 always came up as the magical minimum figure. In Virginia, unlike most states, the charging of fees lower than those set forth in the bar's minimum fee schedule was a ground for disbarment and therefore illegal. Nader and the Goldfarbs decided this was price fixing.

The Goldfarbs then filed suit against the Virginia and Fairfax County Bar Associations. The case eventually went to the United States Supreme Court. That august body sided with the Goldfarb/Nader position. They opined that the setting of *mandatory* minimum fees by Bar Associations was unconstitutional. Virginia's fee schedule was struck down and forever banished.

Although the ruling did not apply to them, associations having only "advisory" minimum fee schedules soon ran scared and fled the scene. Such fee schedules—advisory and mandatory—simply disappeared.

Today's young lawyers now have no guidelines. If they set the sky as their limit then that's their limit. Older lawyers, getting a case the type of which they haven't handled for years, must try to remember what they charged in the good old days. If inclined to go high or low, they will usually go higher than a bar association fee schedule might recommend. The public, not the lawyers, has been hurt by the banishing of such schedules.

The Goldfarbs and Ralph Nader were well-intentioned. There is a certain sin to price fixing, especially if that price is high. But, as is often the case, the well-intentioned cure of one sin led to the unleashing of other, greater sins. Surely, when Dorothy finally flew over the rainbow she expected bluebirds and not captivity by the Wicked Witch of the West. Surely, too, Nader and the Goldfarbs expected the end of minimum fee schedules to be the end of all sins in the field of legal fee settings.

Save for wills, lawyers charge fees according to the time they feel they must spend on a particular case. Since, as Abraham Lincoln pointed out, "Time is the lawyer's stock in trade" (the only item he has to sell), that time must be accounted for. Should a lawyer be charging $70 per hour and he estimates his total time will be ten hours, his fee will be $700. The average lawyer probably spends sixty hours a week at his work. While lawyers might charge $70 per hour, it doesn't always average out this way. They lose some contingent fee cases and thus get nothing. In many instances too, they are left holding the fee bag: the client has skipped town without paying.

Now, in the days of spirited competition in advertising and fee cutting ahead, the general public, trained through TV, newspapers and radio to look for bargains, will gravitate to the lawyer charging the lowest prices. But what of him? He will suddenly be flooded with business. There are only so many hours in a day. A case that should take ten hours from start to finish if it's to be soundly prepared, is now run off in five hours, and the client is short-changed. He got what he bargained for, cut-rate service and, unhappily, perhaps a losing case. The norm prevailing, he might have won. As sure as the sun rises in the east and Jimmy Carter will always love peanuts, cut-rate servicing will come to pass. The game is cutting prices to draw you in. The next game, once you are caught in a retainer contract, is to run your matter off on an assembly line basis so that, quite often, you won't even know what hit you!

The game of fees can also be played by the non-advertiser. He may charge an excessive fee and, with no minimum fee schedule to compare it with, the client will never know he's being "had." Although criminal law fees, in the opinion of many, always appear excessive after time spent has been divided into money received, the minimum fee schedules have kept the vast majority of lawyers pretty well in line down through the years. With the restraint of these schedules gone, even the non-advertising lawyer will find, if he hasn't already, that it is easier to secure a bigger fee now than it was a few years ago before Nader and the Goldfarbs, in doing their good deed, struck down the system.

* * *

What you can do about the fee game

1. Although the day has arrived when lawyers can

advertise actual fees, still shop around to determine what a lawyer charges per hour. Don't take the lowest fee, but an intermediate one. Never ask, "How much does a divorce cost?" for divorces, like houses, come in a wide variety of sizes and prices. A one-room shack (an uncontested divorce with no children, no property, no alimony problems) costs less than a three-story mansion (a contested divorce with every issue known to man involved). The lawyer will have to wait until he hears the facts of a case before he sets a divorce fee; chances are his fee will end up being low, for more unsuspected things arise in a divorce action than in any other kind of lawsuit. He should be able to tell you, by phone, the cost of a will, an adoption, a change of name proceeding, a bankruptcy or the setting up of a small, no-stock corporation, and be able to tell you the percentage fees involved in probate and personal injury cases. If he hems and haws (as criminal law lawyers often do on the phone), go elsewhere. Criminal law lawyers *should* be able to quote fees by phone, but most do not. They want you in the office when quoting their fee. They want to read off to you, in person, the language of the law you violated—remember the fear game discussed earlier?

2. Skim through the yellow pages just to get an idea of the prevailing rates in various fields. *Then immediately disregard lawyers who advertise their fees.* Call lawyers who have not advertised and get their fee quotations. Look for a lawyer whose fees are equal to, or perhaps a bit above, the highest prices you found quoted in the yellow pages. In your legal work it is hoped that you want quality, not a cut-rate product that falls apart on you. Advertisements won't quote high fees because these will frighten bargain-hunters away. But the highest fees shown there will be close to, though still below, what a reasonable fee by a quality lawyer should be.

3. Write to your state legislator asking him to initiate laws allowing bar associations to publish *advisory* minimum fee schedules. The proposed laws should

specifically state that the lawyer charging less than the published fees cannot be prosecuted nor in any way punished by his Bar Association. So long as *Goldfarb v. Virginia, et al* remains on the books a mandatory minimum fee setting would be unconstitutional. The advisory fee schedule would, however, differentiate between the cut-rate lawyer and his reasonable fee brethren.

4. Seek out the reasonable price lawyer. Would you go to a surgeon who charged less to operate on your body simply because he used ordinary home tools—hammer, saw, pliers and steak knives—rather than expensive surgical equipment? Would you go to a lawyer who would operate on only a 50 percent efficiency rate because he had taken on more than he could handle? Whatever your type of case, is it a matter you want to sell on a cut-rate basis to the lowest bidder?

Competition has driven the quality of television sets up and the prices down. In lawyering, conversely, quality invariably lessens when prices start descending. In the one you buy a piece of merchandise, in the other you buy time. Factories can turn out endless pieces of merchandise. Time, unfortunately, is governed by the clock.

CHAPTER 13

Games Played by Government Attorneys

How, you may ask, can attorneys plying their trade for the government play games with the public? After all, it's the general public they represent! Prosecutors prosecute for us, attorneys general protect our consumer rights, public defenders are there to defend us for free if we are too poor to hire a private attorney. As the government says when providing any free service:

"See, it's free! Your government is paying for it!"

Hogwash! Nothing a government does is free. The taxpayer foots the bill. Attorneys working for the government are therefore paid with taxpayer money. The games they may play directly affect your pocketbook. Your taxing authority, be it local, county, state or federal, does not zero in on you as the private attorney did on your bank account a few chapters ago, but you know full well the burden of the overall taxes you bear each year. A penny saved is still a penny earned. So, perhaps, in learning a bit about government attorneys' games, you can prevent such games being played on you, or protest them to your state or federal representatives. Since they (unlike most government attorneys) are elected, they are inclined to listen—and more so to a raging storm of protest than to a whisper.

For the purposes of this book governmentally employed lawyers will be classified into three groups: prosecutors, defenders and those working for state or federal agencies (as opposed to those working for elected officials—the district attorney, state's attorney, etc.).

Prosecutors can be found at every level of government: local, county, state and federal. They may call themselves district attorneys, city prosecutors, attorneys general, state's attorney or whatever names the fifty states may bestow upon them. Their duty is to prosecute criminals. You are the plaintiff in each case (e.g., *The People of the State of California v. Henry Dunwrong, Defendant*). These lawyers rarely play games. Most have more than enough business at all times and, being busy, have little time for games.

A prosecutor's office, for example, may have 500 citizens filing complaints each month, either directly, through police departments or through indictment. Understaffed as most are, they can handle but 300 of these. Two hundred must then go a-begging because:

(a) the evidence was not as strong in their cases as it was in those accepted, and/or

(b) the complaint was not of a serious enough nature. It may have been serious to you but was not as serious as those involved in the 300 filed on.

Prosecutors do, however, play three small games from time to time, all of which have some effect on the general public. The *first* of these are the "crusades" they may carry on for brief periods each year. Crusades may start anytime and involve any crime. Spurred on by a variety of persons—a zealous new presiding judge, the police department, the newspapers or even the district attorney (who is always under pressure from outside sources)—the prosecutor will, for example, vow public vengeance on drunk drivers. There's nothing wrong with that; drunk drivers are a hazard to every community and should be prosecuted. During a "crusade," however, the prosecutor overdoes it. Borderline cases, once filed as reckless driving matters because the evidence did not sustain the burden of proving drunkenness, are now filed as drunk driving matters. At trial time many drunk driving cases are disposed of without trial through the defendant pleading guilty to a lesser offense (e.g., the "reckless driving" that could have been filed on at the outset) or through the offer of an appreciably lower fine or no jail time. During the crusade, however, all deals are off. Plead guilty as charged or go to trial. Since, during these periods, fines are often raised and longer-than-usual jail sentences imposed. most defendants will go to court, hoping to beat the rap. It's the only chance they have, so why not take it? With double or triple the number of cases going to trial the courtrooms become clogged with trials and the courts' calendars begin backing up. Cases not within the scope of the crusade are dismissed or the defendant is given a far better deal in return for his plea than normally would be the case. Worse, a grievous case that would in normal times be among the 300 filed on, is now *not* filed on at all because of the abundance of drunk driving cases filed. During the crusade the prosecutor's "winning percentage"* normally drops because he is trying actions that either should not have been filed or that should have been disposed of by means of a pre-trial plea to a lesser offense. If a crime against *your* person or property was not prosecuted during this period it might well have been because of the "crusade." Though well-intentioned, these crusades are "games" in that after a few weeks or a month or two, they are slowly forgotten and the prosecuting attorney goes back to business as before. Drunk drivers are still prosecuted but only when the evidence is enough to sustain the almost ironclad likelihood of a conviction by judge or jury.

A *second game* played here and there by prosecutors is the filing of every complaint that comes into the office—even those where the evidence is weak, or shaky at most. Those games might arise in a district that is losing population because of an exodus to the city or from the state. The prosecutor is being paid well and has a staff of, say, five assistant prosecutors to help him. He can keep his good pay and entire staff, however, only by keeping up his volume of business. He knows, but doesn't want the public to know, that by not filing on the chaff that comes in he could be obliged to drop one attorney from the payroll.

---

*Prosecutors normally win 90–98 percent of their cases.

Good business *is* slower. His fear, however, is that if he cuts one assistant this year, another will be dropped next year. Eventually the cuts may reach him, if not in person then by a drop in salary. He is not unlike any other governmental head, particularly those found in state and federal agencies. He is entrenched in a nice spot and wants to stay there. Fortunately for the public such games are rare at the grass roots level of prosecution where local crime generally abounds and there are neither police nor prosecutors enough to handle it.

A *third* game played by prosecutors is that of making deals with defense attorneys in return for guilty pleas by their clients. The making of deals is a necessary function of the system because, so long as the judiciary is undermanned and prosecution offices remain understaffed, every case that is filed on just cannot be tried. "Deals" are not as bad as they sound. A man charged with three separate offenses may, for example, be allowed to plead to one and have the other two dismissed. There's nothing wrong in that. The D.A. got his pound of flesh in the plea to one count, for the sentence meted out by a judge for one count is generally the same as for three. "Dealing" is an offense to the public, however, when the prosecutor makes ridiculous deals with defense attorneys. Such deals are concurrent with an over-filing of cases by the prosecutor. A good example occurred several years ago when I visited a courthouse with a client charged with shoplifting. Her defense was flimsy at best. The odds of winning the case weighed heavily against her but she wanted to go to trial. When I arrived at the courthouse I found no less than 102 cases were set for trial that day with only 3 judges available to hear them. Deals, I knew, were going to be made *that* day! When it became apparent to the prosecutor that we were holding out for trial he offered to let us off with a plea to disturbing the peace—the lowest rung of the criminal law ladder.

"We'll take it," I answered for the client, "if no jail time and a suspended fine are involved."

"Agreed," answered the prosecutor with great reluctance. I told my client she was lucky, and she was.

Hundreds of thousands of marijuana users have returned to court time and time again because they were so lightly dealt with after their first arrests. As a result, the "pot cases" have been overcrowding court calendars for years. Not a few prosecutors are in favor of legalizing "grass" if only to give them time to prosecute heavier crimes.

There should be no "easy deals" made by prosecutors. The E-Z deal game hurts you, the public, because the offender is apt to rob, steal or over-drink again. Why not, if he can get off so easily? The public's the loser in this game!

* * *

Defenders play at different games. Games are more prevalent within their ranks than is the case with prosecutors. A "defender" is, by and large, a product of this generation. Before World War II the idea of any U.S. government paying lawyers to defend those too poor to afford their own lawyer was only a dream in the minds of reformers. Somehow everybody could afford a lawyer.

The office of Public Defender came into being in large metropolitan areas after World War II. The defender and his staff defended criminal cases for those who couldn't afford a lawyer. Soon communities unable to afford such offices made lists of local attorneys who would handle criminal defenses for the indigent, sometimes for nothing, but more often for a small fee. In such appointment matters, for example, a private attorney's "going rate" for some case might be $300; the government would pay, say, $100–$500 for the same service. It was better than nothing, particularly for the younger lawyer. For many older lawyers it proved a gold mine. Pressing favors on the clerk or other official who appointed them, they would get a volume of these cases and thereby earn great amounts of money. Several years ago one Los Angeles attorney was found to have earned $68,000 in fees from juvenile court appointments alone. (The commissioner who repeatedly appointed him to such cases was dismissed.) Other examples abound. This is only a game within the community of lawyers, however, for if one lawyer gets $68,000 then ten lawyers, the work spread amongst them, would have received roughly the same amount. No loss to you.

Defender games that cost the taxpayer money are played by the young attorney seeking experience. Be he an attorney on a public defender's staff with cases to try every day, or a new attorney on a court-appointed list who gets an appointment once a month, his primary concern is to gain experience. Many are those on public defenders' staffs who, after a year or two, gain enough experience to go out on their own into private practice. They have learned the tricks of the trade, at the taxpayer's expense.

Before launching into the defender games, let it first be said in defense of public defenders, that the system is a fine one. And many are the defenders who will stay on to make a career of their work. They receive good pay, excellent pensions and medical benefits; they want, and they are entitled to, security. They play at games less because their eye is on a career, not on gaining quick experience so as to go out into private practice.

To gain experience the young and eager-to-get-out-on-his-own defender must try many cases—both jury and nonjury matters. As there is much more to handling a criminal law case than going to trial, he must also experience the many steps that will occur between his client's arrest and the passing of sentence. For experience he must engage in all of these many facets of the criminal case.

At the very outset he is faced with the fact that the prosecuting attorney is winning at least 90 percent of his cases. This is not last year's figure but a year in, year out figure dating back to whenever it was in grandmother's time that statistics were kept on items such as this. This being true, the average defender can then assume that only one out of ten of his clients will be found "not guilty." The probabilities are that his other nine cases will be lost. The experienced attorney will know that he has done a good job if he makes the best deals possible for his defendant-clients as opposed to going to trial. He can steer the case before a lenient judge and "cop a plea," the result for his client being a fine or light jail sentence; the alternative might be to go to trial before a "hanging judge" and see his client sent away to prison. Newspapers never print the heavy losses that nationally famous attorneys such as Darrow, Belli, Bailey or Williams sustain. They print their victories or their "close losses" in spectacular trials (e.g., Bailey in the Patty Hearst defense in San Francisco early in 1976).

Dealing as best he can with any given case does not help the defender gain quick experience. Examples of the game he plays with Mr. and Ms. Taxpayer could be shown as follows:

Step one: He is appointed to represent Jane Caughtinact in a criminal case. He asks for a day's postponement before entering a plea. During this period he studies the police report.

"Drat! She was caught in the act. The state has two eyewitnesses. She later confessed. Just like the two cases I got appointed to yesterday!"

Step two (next day): The defender pleads not guilty on behalf of his client and sets the matter down for a jury trial. In the interim he sets on the court's calendar a motion to suppress evidence. He may have only an inkling as to what evidence he intends to suppress but he might as well make the motion.

Step three: The motion to suppress evidence is denied (as most are). His grounds were weak but he argued strongly and greatly impressed the client who, by now, thinks she may have "a case."

Step four: "Ready for trial, Your Honor."

The courts are clogged so the matter is put over a week or ten days.

Step five: Return for trial. No courtrooms available. Case put on a trailing basis (coming back every morning, day after day, to await the day when some court is ready for the case).

Step six: Finally sent to trial. The trial lasts two days. The jury is out only twenty minutes before bringing in a "guilty" verdict.

Step seven: Defender files a motion for new trial, which gets denied.

Step eight: The defendant, after a probation investigation and report, is sentenced by the judge.

Step nine: The defender, because he needs the experience, files a notice of appeal. He may or may not pursue the appeal, depending on the policy of his office.

While all of this has been going on this same defender has been juggling a dozen or more other cases to which he has been assigned. Jane Caughtinact's case preceded these others so they must wait for hers to conclude before theirs can be tried.

Steps 3, 4, 5, 6, and 9 would have been avoided by the experienced attorney. Why go to trial on a "dead hanger" where the client, under proper circumstances, would have confessed to the police? In such a case the defender could have taken these steps:

Step One: Same as before.

Step two: Enter a guilty plea if there is only one count. If there are two or more counts, work out a deal with the D.A. to dismiss the other counts if a plea is taken to one; this can usually be done. The case is then sent down for probation and sentence.

Interim step three: Out of court. Counsel the client on how to get along with the probation officer she'll be seeing, telling her what to stress, what not to stress. Try for a good probation report.

Step four: The sentence by the court after it has read the probation officer's report.

The elimination of a number of steps in the young defender's presentation of the case would have saved the taxpayers thousands of dollars in lost time. Multiply this sum by the number of times the same type of case occurs daily throughout any state and the figure runs into millions. It doesn't take any attorney, young or old, more than a few criminal cases to become fairly expert at deciding which are the cases suitable for trial, which the one's calling for dealing and pleading.

On one occasion, a year to two ago, I was awaiting calendar call in a local criminal court. Several other attorneys as well as four public defenders were present. None of the four defenders were ready for trial. These were their excuses:

"Not ready, Your Honor. Trailing in six other cases that have priority over this one."

"Not ready, trailing in 13(!) other matters . . ."

"Not ready, trailing in eight . . ."

"Not ready, trailing in nine . . ."

"Trailing" simply means waiting. One had six other cases he had to try before he could try the one being called for trial that day. Add that one and you have seven "trailers." It seemed astounding that the city prosecutor should be filing so many bad cases that everyone was willing to go to trial. Such was not, however, the case. These young defenders were just gaining experience in trying cases. As usual, when all of these cases were completed they won the usual 5–10 percent of trials which defense attorneys are accustomed to winning!

Eventually the local newspaper heard of the tremendous log jam at the courthouse, assigned a writer to it and, after a few articles, matters started going more smoothly. The glaring spotlight of newspaper publicity had done its job. Faced with an unhappy citizenry, Chief Prosecutors and Defenders went back to telling their deputies: settle the losers, try only the winners. The show was back on the road again.

Nor is it easy to spot problems of this sort in juvenile court. There everyone save the minor's parents and witnesses are barred from courtroom hearings. Newspapermen are rarely given the names of the minors involved and just as rarely get stories out of this ever-growing complex of courts. In smaller jurisdictions one judge might handle the community's entire juvenile case calendar in a day, or one judge might be assigned to hear such matters on a day-to-day basis. In larger communities, however, the volume of cases involving minors is rivaling that involving adults charged with crime. In metropolitan areas an intricate system of judges, commissioners and referees gamely try to keep abreast of the myriad juveniles brought before them each day. In such a system, hidden in darkness from the news media, games can be played by lawyers, and are.

The Public Defender system is present in juvenile courts for, as in adult courts, the vast majority of juveniles and their parents are unable to afford lawyers of their own choosing. Defenders here will play at the same game their brethren do in adult court—gaining experience by taking a case the long way round from plea to sentencing. Those who plan to make a career out of public defense work do a better job—taking cases in their stride and gaining experience, as they should, slowly but surely.

The worst of the offenders in juvenile court are those private lawyers appointed by the court to represent indigent minors. In cities where a regular public defender has been established this list of private attorneys is quite lengthy due to conflict of interest cases which the defender cannot handle. Should several minors be arrested for the same crime (e.g., a group of three boys break into a store to burglarize it) the defender may declare a "conflict of interest," stating that he can only represent one of the boys because the versions and defenses involved are in conflict (viz., one lawyer cannot ethically represent both husband and wife in the trial of a contested divorce action and thus a defender cannot represent defendants, minor or adult, whose defenses conflict). A lawyer from the private panel is appointed.

From my observations in juvenile court the game of stretching a case out is played far more often by these private attorneys than by the defender's office. As the county pays them for their time they can, by piling up the hours spent on any given case, amass large amounts of money from this practice. A young attorney friend of mine passed this story on to me:

One day in juvenile court he had been appointed in a certain matter and was handed the file. A reading of the material given him indicated his minor had a bad case. The boy involved had been "caught in the act" and had willingly admitted the crime. My friend talked with the boy who was in court with his mother. He again admitted the offense and both he and his mother said they'd take their "lumps." He'd learned his lesson.

Thereupon my attorney friend told the judge that the boy would admit to the charge (which is, in adult court, pleading guilty). A date was set for sentencing. Upon leaving the court my friend was pulled aside by another attorney, one who, it proved, spent much time in this particular court.

"You are doing this all wrong," the other lawyer told him. "What you do is *deny* the petition at the first hearing, set it down for trial and *then*, when you come back to trial, change your plea if that's what you want. Then they'll set it down for a new date for sentencing. That way you appear three times instead of two and get a larger fee!"

"But the kid was guilty as sin and admitted it," my friend protested.

"That's not the point," he was told. "You should make as much money as you can out of every case!"

I only hope this money-making savant made so much money that year that he had to pay a large tax, a part of which went toward paying lawyers on his panel!

This man's remarks led me to learn of still another game being played by both private attorneys and defenders as well, particularly in large suburban areas. In *all* cases a defender once told me, you should deny the petition and set the case down for trial. Then, on trial day the prosecution witnesses might not show up. This being the case your matter will be dismissed. And the game works! One case I had involved a boy who had had eight prior offenses, on only two of which he had been convicted. The other six had been dismissed because of lack of evidence, to wit, the failure of witnesses to appear. Kids learn fast. This one was obviously keeping his young "life of crime" alive because he could get away with it. In the matter I was handling for him he was "dead" on the evidence but insisted on denying the petition so we could see what happened at trial time. Unhappily for him the witnesses all showed and, though the matter was defended as well as possible, he was convicted. In similar situations juveniles often change their pleas when, on trial day, they see the district attorney's witnesses all present and accounted for. This game may help the minor but certainly hurts society.

* * *

State and Federal Agencies. Devotees of *Reader's Digest* are yearly treated to at least half-a-dozen articles decrying the abuses of federal, and sometimes state, agencies. An "agency" is an administrative body set up by authority of the Congress or state assembly and sometimes the president or state governor. There are so many agencies in existence now that it is doubtful that an exact head count could be made of all of them. They are completely outside the control of the voter, their members being appointed and owing allegiance more to the body appointing them than to the public. They create high paying jobs, and no agency ever established wishes to go out of business once its assignment has been completed. This being the case they perpetuate themselves by continually being busy, busy, busy. If there is no work to be done they find some. Should the purpose for which they are created disappear they create a new purpose. The Federal Corps of Engineers, for example, likes to build dams and is, every year, given money for this purpose. And dams they build whether the public likes it or not. At their current rate of achievement every river in America will boast at least one dam along its course by the year 2000. Rivers be damned . . . and the public too!

As every corporation, criminal mob and city must have its respective staffs of attorneys, so too must agencies have theirs. Whether working on salary with the agency, or on private retainer, the attorney earns good money. Like the agency itself, he would like to keep his job or agency-client. He will help them, in any way he can, to perpetuate the work of whatever agency it is for whom he works.

The game that agency attorneys play is to constantly stir up court litigation and to find new and legal ways for their agency to continue blossoming. An excellent example of the playing of this game was given in a recent *Digest* article by New York's former Senator James L. Buckley:*

"Examples abound illustrating the legal imbalance when a federal agency brings action against private parties," the Senator said. "The Labor Department took a food service firm to court in New Mexico charging that it wrongfully interpreted the overtime and coverage provisions of the Fair Labor Standards Act. The Department lost this case, yet it continued to sue other companies on the same grounds, losing in seven federal district courts and two appellate courts. *After all, it cost a federal agency nothing to lose a case in court.*" (Emphasis mine.)

---

*"*Big Government v. the Little Guy,*" *Readers Digest*, August 1976, p. 87.

It certainly costs the taxpayer a pretty penny, however, to sustain these losses. Senator Buckley pointed out, for example, that the food service companies involved paid close to $100,000 in private legal fees to win these cases.

A man sits at the blackjack table in Las Vegas all day and all night, constantly losing.

"Why do you keep playing when you're losing so much money?" an onlooker inquires.

"Why not?" the player retorts. "Ain't hurtin' me. I got the money to lose!"

Government, it seems, has the money to lose, too, because there is always that steady flow of money into it—the money your taxes provide. Why not play around if the money's there?

The rules and regulations each agency must churn out each year to stay in business are drawn up, in the main, by attorneys. These become law as much as legislation passed by the Congress. The agency OSHA (Occupational Safety and Health Administration) has so many regulations concerning American businesses that only a portion of these rules is contained in a stack of books twelve feet high. And once a rule is promulgated into law the agency, through its attorneys, sees to it that it's enforced! The average businessman has no idea of the total number of all the regulations governing him.

The games which administrative agency attorneys play are entirely dissimilar to anything engaged in by the local, state or federal prosecutor of crimes. The latter, faced with an ever-increasing inflow of business—robberies, rapes, grand and petty thefts, murders, manslaughter, assaults, ad infinitum—have no time to look for new business. As we have seen, they have more than they can handle. On the other hand, if the *Reader's Digest* and other magazine articles are to be believed (and there appears no reason why they should not be), agencies must constantly seek new fields in which their attorneys may sue civilly or prosecute criminally. Limited in the types of cases his particular agency can handle, the administrative attorney must be a kind of inventive genius to find new avenues for work. Should he be unable to do this, and if his well of cases runs dry, he will be out of a job. No one likes to be out of a job, particularly government attorneys (in any field) who are amply paid and nicely provided with fringe benefits.

The defender's or appointed private attorney's game of stretching out a case to unnecessary lengths either for experience (defender) or for more money (appointed attorney) is somewhat akin to the work of the agency attorney. He must constantly litigate to keep his job, and in litigation of the present type of case, as well as in his research, he may find other areas in which suits can be filed. He is, unlike the prosecutor or defender, beyond your control, because his boss is appointed, not elected.

* * *

What you can do about games played by government attorneys

1. There is very little of a constructive nature that you can do about the few games that prosecutors might engage in each year. Their "crusades" in this or that field of crime might well go unnoticed unless your local newspaper reports on the subject. If after several months your prosecutor seems to continue spending more time than he should on prosecuting parking violators, or is prosecuting drunk drivers and letting everything else go, send a letter to the editor of your local newspaper. The newspaper might well start a crusade of its own against this sort of activity. The court system fears the wrath of the newspapers, the glare of its spotlights.

When your prosecutor is running for re-election, look to see if a goodly number of local attorneys are running against him. This is often a sign that the prosecutor is not too well thought of in the lawyering community. The suggestion is not that the prosecutor is rough and tough and lawyers aren't winning enough of their criminal cases, for usually it is the tough-minded prosecutor that lawyers support. Rather, it would be an indication that lawyers in general feel he is not doing a good job for the public. Note also what his opponents say of him in their political ads or newspaper interviews. If most stress certain distasteful traits in the prosecutor which you too find distasteful, then perhaps it is time for a change in that office.

2. You will probably neither read nor hear about games played by defenders or private attorneys appointed and paid by the government. Their fighting of losing cases right through the trial stage can always be charged to "matters of judgment—so we were wrong, so what!" Their games, played in the thousands daily, remain out of the public eye because newspapers cannot keep up with them. The system is too vast, too complex, too fast moving ever to be pinned by even the swiftest of reporters.

Your best chance of besting the game would occur if you were a defendant in a criminal matter or a parent of a minor involved in a juvenile court case. If you, or the child, be guilty and you know it, and you know the case is dead against you (e.g., eyewitnesses, confession after your "rights" were read to you, and/or caught in the act) it is better to get it over with than keep going back and forth to court on pleas and changes of pleas, motions and more motions. Certainly your attorney is gaining experience or earning more money but you as the client are the primary interested party. You are losing your wages and a lot of time by fighting on for a losing cause. Be firm with your attorney. Should he fail to heed you, then "tell it to the judge" when you get to court. It's your case, your freedom, your life that's involved. Question the motives behind your lawyer's insistence that you go to trial in a case that's a sure loser.

"Isn't it because you want to make more money or gain more trial experience?" you could ask for openers.

A number of judges have told me that they are inclined to be harder in sentencing (particularly as to the amounts of fines) when a defendant has wasted the court's time in trying a case that was a dead-bang loser from start to finish. It is generally the inexperienced or money-hungry lawyer who's pushed the case to the limit but the defendant-client is the one who gets hurt.

3. Compiling a list of every federal agency and administrative body in existence would be an exhausting task. If such a list exists it is probably out-of-date because another agency or two may have been formed while the list was being compiled. They constantly play games with the taxpayer's money, but only when the glare of the spotlight hits them will the public be aware of these games.

Contrary to widespread belief, writing your senator or congressman is not just so much wasted time. These elected officials *do* take notice of your complaints and suggestions. A flood of letters pertaining to a certain subject will often lead to congressional action. Write your congressman or state legislator about such abuses. Stress waste in government and the need to cut back in the spending of the taxpayer's dollar on non-necessities. Filing lawsuits hither and yon, for no apparent purpose except to sustain the agency's existence is certainly not "necessary spending." If your local newspapers spotlight such abuses, whether by lengthy discussion or just a small squib, clip it out and mail it to Washington.

Thanks to the proliferation of administrative agencies, the power-in-the-people on which democracy is founded is fast ebbing away. Not elected by the people and often seemingly not responsible to any person or body, these agencies must be watched closely.

The stopping of frivolous lawsuits is but a small part of it, but even a dollar saved here and there helps our depleted pocketbooks at tax time!

CHAPTER 14

The Divorce

Games that lawyers play with your money culminate in one great big game in the divorce case. In the hands of the unethical lawyer such cases may well involve every game you have read about in this book. Like probate matters, divorce cases can drag on for long periods of time and involve large amounts of money. Unlike personal injury cases the money is there throughout the time that the case is pending. Unlike probates the lawyer has direct control of the client's purse strings and need not resort to embezzlement to tap moneys he may be holding.

The "What *is* your fee?" game is the first of those played by the unethical attorney in divorces. Without bar association minimum fee schedule guidelines to go go by he can (and usually does) charge all that the traffic will bear. During your first interview he will secure a good look at your financial picture. This allows him to zero in on your bank accounts. The setting of fees and the going after them go hand in glove for the quick-buck shyster. He will not be the seedy-looking "shyster type" that the movies portray. Slick and well dressed, often seated in a plush office, he defies you to believe he is other than a prosperous, highly ethical lawyer.

Following the example of his criminal law brethren, the divorce case shyster can put the fear of God into husband-clients—or rather the fear that the wife will walk off with all the property and a high alimony award. Only he, our money seeking friend, can save this from happening. The cost will be high (and you'd better believe it!).

Embezzlement is not beyond the derring-do of the unscrupulous divorce lawyer. While he is zeroing in on your bank accounts and finding a myriad legal ways to spend your moneys legitimately, he may also come across large sums of money to hold for you while your case grinds on. House, cars, stocks and bonds may be sold and he, as an attorney of record and an officer of the court,* may be asked to hold the moneys in his trustee-for-clients account. Like his shady probate counterpart it provides him with a fund into which to dip while the case crawls slowly on.

The "low settlement" game discussed earlier, which primarily concerns the personal injury lawyer, is played in the divorce field as the "bad settlement" game. Once the client has run out of money, what is the point in the buck-hungry lawyer pursuing the matter further? None. At this juncture he can, through smooth talk and bewildering legalese, talk the client into a settlement of all of the issues. The settlement may well be, and often is, a bad one from the client's point of view but it serves the lawyer's purpose: it is now settled and he can go on to the fleecing of other clients. "Pull out now and leave the client hanging," is this shyster's credo.

Another game played nationwide in the divorce field is the showering of blandishments on the female client by the dashing male attorney. As she learns to trust him, and sees all he is doing for her, the general dislike she may have had for all men when the case started, slowly disintegrates, at least for this man, her attorney. Offers of cocktails after work, evening dates and weekend dates soon follow. An affair is underway. The client is now emotionally involved with her attorney. She is now easy prey for higher fees, accepting poor settlements and doing, in effect, whatever her attorney bids. Her heart rules her head. The attorney, on the other hand, has been this route before.

---

*A lawyer is considered an officer of the court. As such the representations he makes to the judge are to be believed unless, through experience with particular lawyers, the judge comes to believe nothing *they* say. Until the judge learns of his reputation for unethical conduct, however, any lawyer can get away with much.

He is still controlled by logic. While he may be enjoying this romantic liaison it does not sidetrack him from his primary goal—to make money. On the other hand, should the lawyer-lover become too enamoured of his lovely lady client he may find that emotion is beginning to control the decisions and recommendations he must make along the way. This is just as disastrous for the client. The attorney was hired for his experience, logic and all around knowledge of divorce work. Law is a cold, hard, grinding, logical business dependent on clear thought processes. If these processes are clouded by emotion the case in hand can suffer. Many have.

The "let the client run his own case" game can be used in any field of law by the lazy lawyer but is most often found in divorce litigation. In this game the client decides issues from the outset: how heavy the grounds for divorce should be, how the papers should be served on the opposing spouse,* what to settle for if at all, what witnesses to call at trial time and all the shots in general. The client is sure he knows best. The lazy lawyer, seeing this, figures "What the hell—let him do the work and I'll make the money anyway." The lawyer's gamesmanship lies in the fact that when the client runs matters there is a great deal of wasted time. Since the time is the lawyer's and he charges for it, he often reaps more from this type of client than from one who lets him run the show. If, as is often the case, the matter turns out disastrously at trial the lawyer is protected by the fact that he was only doing what the client asked.

A good example of a client running the complete show occurs at trials of contested actions. The client wants to lower the boom on his/her spouse. The lawyer, if he had his druthers, would rather call a few key

---

*A client of mine once insisted that her husband be served with a divorce Summons and Complaint on Christmas morning, the "papers" tied in a red ribbon and handed to the spouse by a process server dressed as Santa Claus. I talked her out of it.

witnesses—those who saw more, heard more and knew more—than open the floodgates for a score of witnesses who might ramble on and on about minor points. In a tidal wave of witnesses the minor points scored are so plentiful that the major ones, the decisive ones, are often lost at sea. The client who runs his own case usually loses it. Why hire an attorney if you're going to do the work yourself? Let the attorney orchestrate and direct. You be the principal actor. When the play is finally presented the audience will consist of only one person—the judge. The ending is happy only if you draw rave notices from this "audience." Lazy attorneys may be ethical but they're playing games when they let you run your own case.

Attorneys who represent both husband and wife in a divorce suit can often be found playing another game. There is nothing unethical about representing both parties if, and only *if*, they are fully agreed on all issues: alimony, child support, custody, division of property and such other problems as may exist. A final settlement agreement can then be drawn, executed by both of them, and the attorney can thereafter proceed to court with either of them for the simple mechanical procedure of securing the divorce itself. Games-playing enters this situation when the parties, who initially agreed on all issues when first visiting the attorney, decide to differ on one or more important items before a final settlement is effected. If it is apparent the parties cannot resolve their differences the ethical attorney should bow out, sending each spouse to a reputable attorney to handle what will now be a contested divorce case. It's tough when this happens for, although the couple can be charged for the time they took to come to loggerheads, the Big Money lies ahead in the divorce case itself.

The unethical attorney, faced with this loss of future income, succumbs to temptation. He keeps one of the parties as a client and either sends the other to another attorney or, more likely than not, tells him to find his/her own attorney. The unethical games-playing part of such a procedure is that the original attorney now knows a great deal about both sides of the case. Many important and revealing facts have been given to him by each party. Later, at trial, he can use such information against the spouse who gave it to him—the spouse he sent out of the office when the "settlement" disintegrated. Generally he will keep as a client the spouse from whom he is most likely to earn the best fee. Unethical? You bet! But it is being done all across our land by the fee-hungry attorney and will become more common as competition stifles many practices and lawyers must grub for every dollar they can find.

* * *

What you can do about the divorce game

1. Secure a competent attorney at the outset, one who is not known for playing the many games we have discussed. How to do this—through friends, relatives and bar associations—has been earlier discussed in detail.

2. Try to establish and maintain a good rapport with your attorney at all times. Let him run the case and call the shots. If you start fighting and arguing with him he is then in double trouble, having to fight both you and the other attorney. An attorney who must so divide his time cannot do a good job for you. While the opposing attorney zeroes in on winning the case, your attorney must field your complaints and keep you pacified while trying to stave off the other attorney's efforts at the same time. If you just can't stand him and rapport seems completely lost, switch lawyers.

3. Establishing a good rapport with your lawyer doesn't mean going to bed with him or her! Don't get emotionally involved. Social engagements with your lawyer come under the heading of "trick or treat." A

luncheon appointment can be considered a treat.
Pressed for time and/or wanting to discuss matters
with you in a more relaxed atmosphere (clients are
often ill at ease or continually up-tight in a law office),
the attorney's luncheon invitation is generally well
meant and for the good of the case. In the trick category we find the after-work cocktails, evening dates,
suggestions for a weekend in a secluded mountain
cabin, visits to your apartment and little gifts that
might weaken your romantic opposition. "Rapport"
simply means getting along with someone. This can be
done platonically and is best done in this fashion in the
divorce suit.

4. The do-it-yourself divorce craze should be in-
vestigated if yours is a simple, uncontested case.
Many worthy divorce clinics have been set up,
particularly in urban areas, to aid you in such suits
from start to finish. If, for $50–$100, for example, they
can tell you how to process your own divorce, why not
do it in this manner rather than pay upwards of $300 on
an attorney fee for the same mechanical work? If you
and your spouse are arguing about important issues,
however—custody, support, division of property and
the like—it is best to see an attorney. It is all right to
cure the common cold by home remedy but one always sees a doctor for an appendectomy. Divorce
suits also come in all categories, ranging from the
simple to the complex. You must be the judge in this
decision. Saving money is fine and do it when you can.
Saving money but hurting your future in doing so is
something else again.

5. If you and your spouse have reached a settlement agreement on all issues and take the case to one
lawyer, do not under any circumstances allow that
lawyer to take over one side of the case if your settlement breaks down. Report him to the bar association if
he does so. Should he keep your husband's case, for
example, what he learned from you during the initial
interviews could hurt you at trial time. Each spouse
should stalk out and find his/her own attorney in these

situations. If the attorney presses one of you to allow him to keep one side of the case he is showing his un-ethical colors. You don't want *that* kind of attorney for something as important as a divorce can be to you.

CHAPTER 15

Malpractice

Malpractice cases allow attorneys to play games when their clients have cases against "target defendants"—doctors, hospitals, nurses and medical attendants—who carry high-dollar liability insurance. The principal game unethical attorneys play here is to take any medical malpractice suit that comes along and, even though the case may have little legal merit, file suit anyway. Their hope is that the insurance companies will settle these losers for "nuisance value." Such value is described as an amount equaling a few dollars less than it would cost the carrier to fight the suit through a jury trial. If, for example, a carrier estimates that it will take $5,000 in attorney fees, court costs and investigation expenses to complete a case, it might be interested in settling for four bills, a savings of $1,000. Attorneys, having played the nuisance value game for centuries in many types of lawsuits, play it in medical practice suits too. For some years it was quite easy to secure settlements on this basis.

But slowly the worm was turning. By the early 1970s insurance companies were, more often than not, fighting these nuisance value suits through trial. Doctors and hospitals were beginning to win more verdicts. Doctors who disdained the high costs of malpractice insurance would, if sued on poor liability cases, defend the suits with their own money. No settlements for them in cases where they felt they were in the right!

It is difficult to estimate how many medical malpractice cases can be classified as merely "good" or "bad." One prominent California attorney specializing in medical malpractice, estimates that only three out of ten clients he sees with complaints in this field have cases worthy of filing. The other seven involve

people who got bad results after medical treatment
and/or hospitalization and thus figure they have a suit.
Their theory: if I wasn't cured, the doctor must have
slipped up. The law, unfortunately for them, requires
the doctor or the hospital and its employees to have
acted negligently (without the due care and diligence
proper to a physician) or willfully (purposely commit-
ting a wrongful act on a patient). If a doctor did his
best and the patient still died, his heirs would have no
suit. But nowadays the tendency is that if a person
dies his heirs sue; if a person becomes crippled after
an accident and the doctor does not un-cripple him, he
sues. Everyone sues!

As there are hundreds of thousands of doctors
across the nation and millions of medical situations
arising each year, the law of averages dictates that
some doctor, nurse or hospital will, here and there,
commit malpractice. Ethical attorneys take these
cases, and turn down the losers. Attorneys after a
quick buck take the losers hoping for either:

    (a) a nuisance value settlement or,

    (b) a miracle at trial, to wit, a jury who will give
them a verdict.

I have talked to a number of ethical malpractice attorneys about clients who come to their offices with
matters in this field of practice. All have assured me
that, at most, only three out of every ten "cases" that
are presented to them are worth filing in court. The
other seven have invariably fallen into that trap of
popular misconception—the trap that wrongly opines
that if the medical result is not perfect then it follows
that the doctor can be sued.

As the public learns that the medical profession will
fight bad cases right through to the end, it will slowly
back away from suing the doctor in every instance.
Part of the gamesmanship in unethical attorneys encouraging clients to sue the medical profession even
when the case is a poor one from the client's point of
view lies in *not* telling the client that, if he loses the
case, he must not only pay his court costs but also

court costs for the other side. These can amount to staggering sums in malpractice cases, jury fees, reporters' fees on depositions, witness fees and a conglomeration of smaller costs all adding up to a total of thousands of dollars. Attorney fees are not chargeable as costs, but should be.

But there are many kinds of malpractice. The type now beginning to blossom will remind writers and readers of short stories that use the "biter bit" plot. It's the case of the trickster who finally falls victim to his own trickiness, of the bad guy who wins all the way until he steps into the trap he himself has set. "Hoist by his own petard" is a commonly used expression to describe the situation. Is the shyster the biter who will be bitten?

Yes, indeed he is! A glimpse of his fate may be seen in the following headlines in a recently published newspaper:

ONE MILLION DOLLAR LEGAL MALPRACTICE
SUIT FILED AGAINST TWO LAWYERS

* * *

CLIENT FILES SUIT FOR MALPRACTICE:
ASKS $75,000.*

In the same newspaper a headline not implying malpractice spoke of a lawyer who sued a client he was currently representing in other matters. He was up to his ears in malpractice claims both from this client and from the others he was representing!

A decade ago a few of these stories appeared several times a year; now they appear weekly. A score of years ago suits against lawyers were minimal in number, today they are growing. People who yesterday were suing their doctors for bad results period (as op-

---

*The story was of an ex-client suing his former attorney for negligently handling his case.

posed to bad results caused by negligence) are now turning on lawyers with such suits. If a case be lost— criminal, civil, divorce or otherwise—the attorney "loser" stands a better chance of being sued for malpractice, whether he "malpracticed" or not, than he did a generation ago. There is an old joke among attorneys that when a client wins he exclaims, "*I* won, *I* won!"; when he loses he looks at the lawyer and says, "*You* lost, *you* lost!" The joke isn't so funny anymore.

Attorney James Sutherland, a domestic relations law specialist, writing in the September 1976 issue of the Long Beach (California) *Bar Bulletin* warns lawyers that a malpractice wind is blowing in the direction of those handling divorce cases. Laws and rules concerning this type of case are in a constant state of flux and the attorney must keep abreast of the constant changes in the law or face the possibility of malpractice at suit's end. Sutherland is right. In no other field will attorneys themselves be more prone to fall victim to malpractice suits than in the field of divorce. At suit's end both parties are invariably upset with the court's decision (except in the soon-to-be-extinct situation where one gets all of the property and exactly as much support as wanted). On one occasion I secured a court order for a woman client wherein she got 80 percent of her husband's total income for support of herself and one child. Satisfied? No indeed! She turned to me and bitterly asked, "Why couldn't I get it all? I certainly need it!"

Even divorce cases that are settled before trial can lead to malpractice problems. Never have I seen an agreement where, one day later or a year later or somewhere in between, one of the parties doesn't become sorrowful at having entered the agreement. The stock the husband got by way of the agreement goes down while the wife's home increases in value. He gets mad and turns his wrath on the attorney for not having held out longer or, at least, insisted that both home and stock be split fifty-fifty. The lawyer reminds the client that he, the client, wanted the home/stock division the way it was written up and has no one but himself to blame. The client, however, has conveniently forgotten.

Games unethical attorneys play in divorce cases, may well come back to haunt them in the form of malpractice suits. Even if they don't play games, they must mind their P's and Q's and strictly guard against negligence since, like ethical lawyers, they too can be sued.

The game of the malpractice suit of little merit filed against a doctor for a quick buck can boomerang on its perpetrator, who may find *himself* being sued. Biter bit? You bet!

* * *

What you can do about the malpractice game

1. I have always favored the "English rule" that the winning party (except in criminal cases) be awarded attorney fees in every instance. Today, unless there's a contract calling for such awards, or a law requiring the losing party to pay such fees (as there is in too few states) the "American rule" is that each side, win or lose, pay his/her own attorneys.

The payment of the winner's attorney fees by the loser would discourage frivolous lawsuits. Malpractice suits filed for "nuisance value" would become a thing of the past. Suits that might now be settled just as trial begins but which are not (because of the thought, "What have we got to lose by going to trial?") *will* be settled.

The salient feature of an attorney fee order is that such fees run far, far higher than a combination of the winners' and losers' "court costs." In big cities a reputable, big-time insurance company defense attorney may draw $500 per day for trial time. Simple mathematics show that a ten-day trial will bring him a $5,000 fee. The average man, filing a bad case, would have a tough time finding this kind of money when, after losing the case, he is ordered to pay fees in addition to court costs. Bankruptcy? Probably.

You can help by bombarding your state assemblyman or congressman with demands to have the "English rule" written into law. Since we have copied much of our law from Mother England, it would not be too difficult to adopt this law. Opposition will come from the "gambling attorneys" (of whom there are many) who will file so-so cases just for the chance of winning. Some file on a volume basis, expecting they will win perhaps 10 out of 100, but knowing they will make a profit just the same. However, rather than wasting the court's time (your taxpaying dollars) in filing ninety losers "just for the chance," they should be more selective at the outset. The loser-pays-the-fees rule would cut down much litigation in America, unclog the overburdened court system and allow the courts to devote more time to the good cases. The latter are now caught in the current morass of cases which require a wait of sometimes five years before going to trial. Ethical attorneys would also be protected by the rule. Willy-nilly suits against them for "malpractice" would subside too. Only the winners would be filed upon.

2. If you have a medical malpractice case don't seek the advice of friends on this occasion, but go directly to your bar association for referral to a *reputable* attorney who *specializes* in such matters. If *he* tells you you don't have a case, believe him. Why should he lie to you? His fee would be contingent on your winning; if you won he would make a good fee. He feels, however, that you would lose and thus he would make no fee. If you had such a good case (you certainly thought it good enough to take to an attorney), wouldn't he take it if he *too* felt it was worthy of eventual recovery? Of course he would. If you still don't believe him, go back to the bar for referral to another attorney. A second or third opinion, *from an attorney who knows what he's talking about,* will be

your best bet. Don't go to a divorce specialist who's never handled a medical malpractice case in his life, nor a criminal defense or bankruptcy specialist. What do they know? Again, who knows but they might take your case just for the chance at a fast dollar? Others may be planning a trip to Lourdes in the near future and will take your case so that a successful conclusion of your case can be one of the miracles they pray for.

Think twice, also, about filing a malpractice case when, on the advice of several attorneys, you are told you don't have a very good case. Should you find some attorney to file for you (and you will if you keep looking!) your pocketbook and bank account might be emptied along the way in paying for court costs. All that time wasted, a zero jury verdict, and $2,500 in court costs to pay!

3. If you are unlucky enough to be involved in a contested divorce case don't expect miracles. Don't expect anything to end up exactly as you'd hoped it would. Thanks to the current movement for equality of the sexes, both men and women are, more and more, beginning to be treated as equals by the court. When I became a lawyer in 1948, women could almost "write their own ticket" in divorce cases, particularly in community property states. I saw, in my own early practice that wives were walking away with, on the average, 75 percent of the total community property in contested divorce matters. Division of property was predicated to a large extent on the seriousness of the "grounds." Women seemed always able to present the better grounds and thus got more property. In handling a thousand and more cases for women clients I found out the why of this. It was simply that women do, now as then, have minds like traps. They could, in going over grounds, remember incidents from their honeymoon night and, after proceeding day by day down to the present, (a thirty-year marriage sometimes required hours of interviewing to get the total grounds!), they had plenty of ammunition for the trial. Men, on the other hand, had vague recollections

of this or that but fell back in the main on generalizations such as "She nagged a lot." (Reply: Why not? The bum drank and chased women all the time" [enumerating ten dozen instances]). Or the man might say, "She spent all my money." (Reply: "All I spent was what little he had left over after drinking with the boys on payday!") According to a startling California statistic of some years ago, among men over fifty-five years of age, the divorced men committed suicide at a rate three times greater than all other men in the group. The "new divorce law" of 1970 required equal division of community property by the court and by the end of 1973 that suicide rate had returned to normal. A divorced man over 55 now took his own life no more, no less, than other such men. Wiped out in olden days by a wife getting 75–100 percent of the property, these older men were unable to face starting life over again, and so took the tough way out.

4. Think twice, then, and more than twice, about suing your attorney for malpractice in divorce cases. Again, get the opinion of two or three reputable attorneys—as you did in the medical malpractice case—before filing suit. Nobody "wins" a divorce case.

CHAPTER 16

Adoptions

Adoption cases fall into three basic categories: step-parent, agency and independent.

The step-parent adoption is one in which a husband adopts as his own child, his wife's child or children by a previous marriage; the wife can, of course, adopt the husband's children but the former occurs more frequently. In every case, should the child's other natural parent be alive, his or her formal consent must be obtained before a court will grant the adoption. The big step and only problem in these cases is securing that consent. Should this require abandonment proceedings (because the other parent has abandoned the child and, you claim, his consent is therefore unnecessary) or lengthy correspondence or conferences with the consenting parent, then the attorney is justified in charging more. The ethical practitioner will determine in advance whether it appears likely, or otherwise, that the consent will be given. No formal consent can be given until the adoption suit is filed but the strong probabilities of a consent being either given or withheld can be determined before filing. The unethical lawyer will be more inclined to file suit immediately, thus securing a good portion of his fee, and then find out that no consent can ever be obtained, viz. that the other parent will not give his/her consent and has not legally abandoned the child. This lawyer will huff and puff and spend more time, but your suit will die aborning. Investigate the consent aspects yourself before seeing the attorney.

The agency adoption occurs where a duly licensed adoption agency has given you the child. Long before the child comes to your home, eventually to be yours, the agency has secured the necessary consent from the child's parents, or, as is often the case with unwed mothers, the mother alone. Compared even to the usually minimal-work step-parent adoption, there is little work for the attorney to do in the agency case. If the lawyer has never had an agency case before, the agency will have forms he can use for filing the petition, getting the court order and anything else that state law may require. They will outline for him the steps he must take from start to finish. Your fees here should be low. In most cases the agency will recommend one or more attorneys to you. You are generally assured in such cases that these named attorneys

(a) know what they're doing and

(b) will charge modest fees. After all, if they foul matters up or charge exorbitant prices the agency will strike their names from the list. There goes another source of business. No lawyer wants *that*! Without such a recommendation you are on your own. If the attorney you finally select is unknown to you he may, within the narrow confines allowed in the agency case, confine his game to charging larger fees or creating unnecessary work. He won't have time to zero in on your bank account and there'll be no palaver about the possibility of your having a "bad case." The agency has told you otherwise.

Independent adoption involves you in finding your own child—not one from an agency, not your spouse's by a previous marriage. Being the longest, hairiest- and most trouble-fraught of all types of adoption it is the one in which your games-playing attorney will be most likely found. Some of the games he may play are these:

1. Should he, through a doctor friend or otherwise, find a baby for you he may charge a lump sum that is tantamount to a "finder's fee." This tactic is illegal in all states and if you go along with it you will at least have the knowledge throughout the entire case that you are dealing with a shyster.

2. Should *you* have found the baby the lawyer can spend a lot of time talking the mother into giving her consent (he says!) and time, as always, is the lawyer's

stock in trade. Most states require an okay of the independent adoption by some state-controlled adoption administration. The games-playing lawyer can wrangle with, or otherwise fail to cooperate with, the adoption administration so that, when its final report is filed with the court, it *disapproves* the adoption. This, in effect, means the state is contesting the case and a long battle lies ahead. By provoking the adoption administration to a disapproval the lawyer has made more money for himself. He can do this with some degree of safety because the adopting parents win the vast majority of these contests. Still and all, once a disapproval is filed, they must shell out more money to reach the end of the legal road.

3. He may, right off the bat, play the bad-case game with you. You, never having adopted a child before, don't know the problems, pitfalls and legal gremlins that lie in your path. He will extract from you a larger fee than you should have paid.

Should the lawyer you select eagerly accept your independent adoption case, you run the risk of his being a games-player. Many lawyers, once they are established, no longer take independent adoptions. These cases probably run a close second behind divorces in types of practice lawyers abandon after they've been in practice awhile or entrenched in a firm where younger lawyers can take these heartbreakers. While many "independents" run through smoothly, just as many can turn out to be real headaches. In the worst of them you walk a tightrope all the while carrying nature's most precious gift—a human baby. Should the natural mother not give her consent, or should the court refuse the adoption, the child is lost forever to the clients who have had him in their home for a year or more. Tears follow tears and it's heartache time.

Although I successfully handled many independent adoptions in the fifties, I was wearing out by the time the 1960s rolled around. In one of my last cases a 48-year-old woman and her 66-year-old husband had found a baby to adopt. There was no problem on consent from the natural parents. The final report of the state, however, disapproved the adoption. My clients were too old by state standards. Since their standards were not law, the adoption could go through if we won the contest.

The case took two days to try. Much of the time was taken in the testimony of one of the city's leading doctors of internal medicine to whom I had sent the 66-year-old father-to-be (it was he, primarily, to whom the state objected). The doctor had examined the man at length and found him to be as fit as a fiddle—"as healthy as any forty-year-old," were his words. The court allowed the adoption to go through and the judge told me later that the doctor's testimony had won the case for me.

"It was a very close case," he said, "and if you hadn't had that doctor I wouldn't have granted the adoption."

In the end, however, the adoption agency turned out to be correct in its original analysis. The now 67-year-old man died of a sudden heart attack two months to the day from the granting of the adoption. The child, less than a year old, would grow up fatherless.

My final adoption before saying goodbye to this field of legal endeavor involved a natural mother who failed to give her formal consent. Over the years, in such cases, I had always had a long conference, and sometimes two or three, with the natural mother before filing the Petition for Adoption. I wanted to feel as certain as one can get that she would sign her consent when, after filing, the time came. Most were no problem at all. Several I had reservations about but they gave their consents. On two occasions I told the prospective parents that I was certain that the mother would eventually refuse to consent. It was only a "gut feeling" but that was my opinion. In both of these cases the clients went to other attorneys. In both cases suit was filed and, as I predicted, the mother refused to give her consent and recovered her child in each situation. Luck, or whatever it was, eventually ran out on me. In my final case the mother withdrew her consent as the case approached adoption day. She had seemed as reliable at the outset as the many girls before her who had consented, but something came along at a later date to make her change her mind. The heartbreak of the adopting parents in losing the child, mingled with the joy of the mother in finding a way to keep the child, was as traumatic an experience for me personally as I can remember. To save going through it again I gave up "independents."

Should the lawyer you seek out not handle independent adoptions ask him to refer you to a competant lawyer who does still take them. Hoping you'll come back to him when you have another type of case in the offing, he'll undoubtedly refer to someone he can trust and who knows his business.

What you can do about the adoption game

1. In any of the three adoption matters discussed, your bar association still remains your best bet for selecting an attorney. Most will refer lawyers by their specialties and those who have listed "adoption" have generally had enough of these cases to be experienced. If in doubt the bar association can always advise you how long the attorney has been in practice. This has little bearing on agency and most step-parent adoptions, however, since one can "go by the book" in these.

2. Seek out people you know have adopted children and find out the name of the lawyer they used. If their reports are satisfactory see the lawyer they used. There is no better recommendation than a satisfied client.

3. In agency adoptions get as much information from them as possible before seeing a lawyer. Agencies should know the standard rates in the community for this type of case. They can outline for you

the very few steps involved. They can tell you of the many forms they have and of the help they'll give your attorney. Armed with this information, you can stalk out of the games-playing lawyer's office the moment he says ''tough case—a thousand dollars.''

4. In independent adoptions make certain the lawyer you retain will talk to the parent or parents whose consent is necessary before the case can conclude. Make certain he talks to them before suit is filed. Although he cannot be faulted for guessing wrong, (and it is only a guess until it becomes fact) he may find he has a loser on his hands before he starts. In such a case the suit shouldn't be filed.

CHAPTER 17

The Psychology of It All

Students will sometimes come up to me after class to announce their intentions of going on to law school once their college days have ended. They are interested in what pre-law classes I would recommend their taking. I usually try to dissuade them from such a career, pointing out that orthodonture would bring greater financial rewards, the ministry more peace of mind, but none are dissuaded. They plunge onward. What college courses would I recommend?

In a poll I ran some years ago, most lawyers considered *English* to be a fundamental "must" for those who would practice law. A few courses in *accounting* would serve the would-be lawyer well; even if he did not plan to practice tax law the taxes *he* must pay and the office records *he* must keep, stagger the imagination of one who has never had any training in this field. *History* was the number one recommendation for pre-law students in the first half of this century. I majored in the subject and later secured a master's degree in it. Much as I enjoyed history, however, it does little to help me in the everyday practice of law.

Psychology is something else again. Most students, pre-law or otherwise, will take a course or two in psychology just because it appears to be, as it is, an interesting elective. Few planning to be lawyers will realize how important psychology will be to them after they finally pass their bar exams and hang out their shingles to practice.

A solid understanding of psychology proves, over the years, to be the very backbone of a law practice. The craft of lawyering is probably made up 25 percent of law, 25 percent of facts and 50 percent of psychology. The young lawyer will learn it swiftly and understand its importance early in his career. It is the key to his understanding judges, juries, insurance adjusters, witnesses, court clerks and, most importantly, you, the client. "Reading" the personal injury case client differs from understanding the person involved in a divorce case. The criminal law client may be a person with a long previous record or he may be a first-time offender. Knowing how each will "tick" will prove of great assistance to the lawyer.

Psychology in its simplest definition is the science which predicts the behavior of individuals (e.g., clients) and groups (e.g., juries) through understanding their underlying abilities and motives. Through the art of prediction one learns how to control these persons.

What motivates your client? What is his basic emotional drive, his intellectual perception, his strengths, his handicaps? Does he come on strong, or is he weak? Will he try to bull his way through the case or, like a lamb, will he follow your lead? The answers to such questions will be forthcoming to the well-trained lawyer soon after the client's case is undertaken. It is imperative that the lawyer understand his own client. He is the hub around which the case will revolve.

It is also imperative that the lawyer understands judges and juries. These people will ultimately decide your client's case. Melvin Belli, the highly successful San Francisco attorney, is a master of psychology, particularly in relation to juries. He has written many books on various aspects of law and all are loaded with the psychological aspects of legal practice. Read one if you get the chance. Trier of far more jury cases than a dozen average lawyers will collectively try in their lifetimes, he can explain the psychology of a trial far better than I can.

The fact is the lawyer is far more likely to plumb the depths of his client's psyche than vice versa. This is all well and good if the lawyer is ethical. Knowing a client as well as understanding the psychology of the law business will aid that client's case greatly. Should his client be a heavy drinker, for example, he would down-play this issue in a divorce case. Expecting the other party to bring it up at the time of the trial, however, the lawyer might prevail on his client to join A.A. This surprise would be helpful at trial-time. Judges admire people who have seen the light and become better citizens for it.

A young attorney friend of mine had a case in which an ex-husband was accused of setting fire to his ex-wife's auto. One piece of advice I gave him was to get as many divorced men as possible on the jury. Perhaps one among them would say to himself during the course of the trial, "Gee, I'd do the same thing myself if I had the chance." From years of divorce work I knew that many people, men and women alike, remained vindictive even years after their divorces. Since my friend had a relatively bad case (one fairly good eyewitness for the prosecution and another who placed the defendant in the vicinity at the time of the fire) it was just as well he tried to "hang" the jury. After finally being able to seat three divorced men in the jury box, he went to trial. The jury hung at eleven to one. The "one" was a divorced man. Rather than try the case again the district attorney allowed the defendant to plead guilty to a lesser charge. It was a victory of sorts and largely dependent on the psychology of a given situation.

Sadly for you, the shyster lawyer is a master of psychology too. Consider the good-case, bad-case game that led off this book of games. The lawyer's manipulations there are completely based on the use of psychology. From experience he knows what to say and when to say it. He leads you through a mental maze until at last you sign up with him and on his terms. Your only defense is having the will-power to get up and leave without signing anything.

Return to our Table of Contents. Review the chapter titles. Each and every one of these games lawyers play is based on a knowledge of psychology and how to apply it. The unethical criminal lawyer scares you half to death by reading you the exact language of the law you have allegedly violated; this makes you easy prey for the higher fee he'll demand. The ambulance chaser is a master of sweet-talking you into signing up with him, psychology again. There is also the right moment in every case to zero in on your bank account or to embezzle outright from funds the lawyer is holding for you; the "right moment" is when your counsel knows he has you under control, off-guard and completely unsuspecting. Advertising, whether by lawyers or anyone else, is a 100 percent psychological appeal. James Coburn sold a lot of beer and Joe Namath a ton of panty-hose because their fans flocked to buy these items. Would you buy a hamburger if Fidel Castro recommended it or would you be more inclined to buy one if Rodney Allen Rippy grinningly asked you to visit Jack-in-the-Box? Psychology.

Study lawyers' newspaper, TV and radio ads during the next few years. While the present ones are fairly bland (awaiting the edicts the of state bar associations on what is or is not "proper" advertising), later ones will most likely make a heavy appeal to your emotions and social values. Many an attorney has already built a solid clientele on the "free advertising" he gets from the news media when he represents movie stars, sports figures or other celebrities.

"My attorney represents (naming a glamorous movie actress)," a friend tells you, pride gushing from her every pore.

That makes him a good lawyer?

Ad men know what appeals to the masses, the potential buyers of his clients' products, and by understanding them can make buyers out of them. Advertising is 90 percent psychology, 10 percent sheer guts. The man who knows the public and has the guts to parade Joe Namath around in panty hose, will be a winner.

Lawyers will be advertising winners too. As they must master psychology to be successful in the law business, the art of persuading the public to visit their offices is a talent already theirs. Trial lawyers, the der-ring-do experts of the profession, should come up with some sensational ads. He whose business it is to make silk purses from sows' ears will have little trouble catching the public's eye. Advertising is, after all, only the arousal of public desire to buy this product or that service. Psychology.

Bates and O'Steen were among the pioneers in opening legal "clinics." When they opened their of-fices in Phoenix they knew the public had learned to believe "clinic" meant high quality service at lower rates. The success of medical clinics had paved the way for them. One would always be charged less in such a clinic than in the swanky offices of a solo prac-titioner. Although the state bar of Arizona took um-brage at Bates and O'Steen over their clinic, and over their temerity in advertising its existence, the United States Supreme Court did not. Psychology set them up and the advertising they received from the final court decision was invaluable.

Lawyers have always been infamous for the flowery language they use—big words, Latin words, incalcula-bly unidentifiable words. The psychology of such language is to dazzle the lay client and keep him con-stantly in awe of his attorney. This language game has a remote, but still viable, connection with sometimes overcharging the client. Should the attorney note that the client is greatly impressed by his lawyer's vocabulary, he may big-talk his way to a larger fee.

Don't be impressed by the big-word barrister. When he has completed a Spiro Agnew-like delivery of words, calmly ask him to reduce what he said to simple English. Never be embarrassed to ask. It's your money, your case. You are entitled to have everything explained to you in simple language. If he continues to speak in mysterious terms, pull out and secure the services of a simple English-speaking law-yer. Chances are that in these days and times Mr. Big Word may be trying to cover his ignorance.

My old friend Jim Hayes, now a Los Angeles

County Supervisor, fathered California's "new divorce law of 1970." I know he wanted to keep its language simple. Though he succeeded to a great degree, a so-called "blue ribbon panel" of California divorce attorneys pressured through the exact language that would secure a dissolution-of-marriage for the party seeking one.

"During your marriage have irreconcilable differences arisen between you and your spouse which have led to the irremediable breakdown of your marriage?" the attorney now asks his divorce-seeking client on the witness stand.

If the client has been coached ahead of time he or she will answer "yes." On the other hand, if not warned of this language in advance, the client will often say "no" (especially women who, it seems are always raised as children to always say "no" when a man asks them a question they don't understand!)

How much simpler it would have been had this language been allowed by the law:

Attorney: "Do you and your husband/wife get along?"

Client: "No."

Attorney: "Is your marriage past saving?"

Client: "Yes."

But hard-core groups of lawyers, found in every State, are dedicated to the proposition that the language of the Law must remain mysterious. Fortunately this profound, enigmatic and often inexplicable wordage is dying out as people come more and more to demand simple, straight-arrow language. But the death of such talk will be a long and slow one. Lawyers don't give up easily!

What you can do about the psychology game

Finding a lawyer speechless is tantamount to finding another Hope Diamond. Here, however, you find me speechless if your endeavor is to determine how you can match psychological wits with your lawyer. He is the master of the game and this may well be your first case. Even if this is your fifth case, your lawyer is probably ahead of you by several thousand. The one person who comes closest to learning the psychology of the lawyering business is the criminal who is before the bar of justice for, say, the twentieth time. He will know the score. Many of these, knowing the score, represent themselves. They may lose the case but they know a lawyer might lose it too. The D.A., you'll recall, wins 95 percent of his cases.

My best advice is to apply the old saw "an ounce of prevention is worth a pound of cure." Throughout this book it has been repeatedly suggested that you secure a competent, ethical, non-shyster-type lawyer in the first place. Securing one of these, whether through a bar association or the recommendation of friends, you will not be required to match wits with him. His wits and knowledge of psychology will aid you, rather than hurt you, as the case proceeds. If yours is a personal injury case there is an art to dealing with insurance adjusters—the men who have the money you want. In divorce work knowing the other attorney and what to expect of him is perhaps the most important ingredient. And so it goes, your attorney using psychology to your advantage.

Should you secure an attorney by the pot-luck method, however, or find a bad apple in the barrel of attorneys the bar association recommended, you can only be on your guard to recognize some of the games he might play. Bad-mouthing your case at the initial interview but then reluctantly agreeing to take it, is your tip-off that the bad-case game is being played on you. Big monthly bills from your attorney, in what you thought was a simple case, may be a warning that your bank account, not you, is your lawyer's primary consideration. Consistent failure on your attorney's part to inform you of what is happening in your case may be a clue that nothing is happening. All talk and no action; fee paid but no work done.

If you have secured the services of what proves to be one of the bad guys, don't hesitate to cut out and seek help elsewhere. Too many people are inclined to believe that once they've signed on with an attorney they can't back out. Nonsense! There is no attorney contract that is permanently binding on you. Dissatisfied, you can always walk away. You may owe moneys for services the attorney has rendered to date but, if you feel his charges are too high, you can always force him to sue you in the courts. Surprisingly few sue and those who do often find their charges cut down to some extent by the trial judge.

Psychology is, after all, a science that all of us know and use to a large degree during our business and social lives. Some of us use it for good purposes, some for bad. How your attorney uses it will depend on his ethics. Secure an honest one at the outset. In so doing you'll know psychology will be used as an asset, not as a game.

CHAPTER 18

The Specialists

Few doctors today are general practitioners in the old-fashioned sense of the term. Tiptoe through the yellow pages of your local phone directory; see how doctors specialize. Note that "general practitioners" are more often than not associated with clinics; if a problem proves beyond their capabilities these doctors can refer the patient to specialists who, invariably, also have offices in those clinics.

Lawyers have been slightly slower than medical men to realize their world is also becoming one of specialization. The lawyer who tells you he is able to handle any kind of case that comes along is either kidding you or kidding himself. An exception would be the very young lawyer. He can have a general practice because he has no practice at all.

My very first case was a simple bankruptcy. Since it was a month later before I had my second client, I considered myself somewhat of an expert on bankruptcy. I read laws, cases and textbooks on the subject. My reverie of starting a bankruptcy empire was shattered with the appearance of my second client. She was a defendant in a contested divorce matter. Within a few days I was well on my way to learning everything I wanted to know about divorces and what to do with the knowledge. The opposing lawyer had an office in northern California. Each day, having nothing else to do after reading myself dry on divorce law, I would write him a letter discussing the case. After thirty days and thirty letters he caved in and settled the case on our terms. My client was so happy she referred a girl friend for a divorce. I was suddenly a "divorce expert."

Business got better, as it always did for the young lawyer in those days. Personal injury, criminal and civil cases followed. By the early 1950s I realized I was a "general practitioner." Life then was easier, laws fewer and pressures less than is the case today. Should some client bring me a matter I had never handled before it was a simple task to bone up on the law and take the case to conclusion. Patents and other high-specialty matters I had learned to send on to the specialist.

The winds of change, blowing stiffly in the sixties, reached tornado proportions in the 1970s. It occurred to me one day circa 1969 that the California Codes (books of laws passed by the legislature) seemed to have doubled in size since I'd started practice twenty years previously. A brief survey indicated I was right. Every year millions of new laws, rules and regulations are passed by Congress, legislatures, councils, and administrative agencies across the nation. On the other hand, few laws are repealed. With the constant addition of new laws and the resultant court decisions that necessarily follow close behind, various fields of law—simple to practice in days of yore—turned into "specialties." Many lawyers doggedly clung to the idea that they were general practitioners, however, and burned the candle at both ends in a valiant attempt to keep abreast of the law and its almost monthly, sometimes daily, changes.

Given my druthers, I'd have chosen personal injury, agency adoptions or juvenile court work as my specialty. The lawyer out on his own, though, has no real choice. He turns into an expert in that type of case that most oftens comes through his door. When it became apparent to me that the days of general practice were in a comatose condition, I realized that, if anything, I must be a "divorce expert." Eighty percent of my income was derived from this field and one client always seemed to send in one or two more. Although I did the best work I was capable of doing in this field, and enjoyed many phases of it, it was (and is) the most stressful of all branches of practice. The pleasure of reconciling a couple or of reaching an amicable settlement early in their divorce proceedings was more than offset by the many who fought on to the bitter end. With the arrival of the 1970s there seemed to be fewer reconciliations and settlements, far more dogfights. If the world has seemed stormy in this past decade, nothing in it has seemed stormier than the area of divorce. My heart twice told me to stop and on the second occasion I believed it. Save for settled-ahead-of-time divorces I wouldn't touch one now with a ten-foot pole. To each his own choice, but mine, primarily, is working with and for young people.

When you go shopping for a lawyer seriously study the type of case you are going to present to him. If it's an uncontested divorce or a "no assets" bankruptcy, a minor criminal matter or a change-of-name proceeding, the G.P. may be your man. His charges will tend to be less than the specialist's at that. If your case is not in any of these minor categories, however, seriously consider getting the specialist. Our local bar association has a list of twenty-three specialties from which the would-be client can select an attorney. When I started practice, twenty-three would have been a ridiculously high number. Today it is not.

A few of the specialists you may wish to employ are these:

Patent & Copyright Law:

This is a highly specialized field. Those who practice it do nothing else. My most urgent advice is to seek out the specialist if you have something to patent or copyright. A games-playing attorney might be inclined to tell you, "Sure, I can handle copyrights," but you won't know if he's ever handled one in his life. He can bone up on it after taking your matter but it will cost you twice as much (you pay for his research time into a field that is virgin to him) and take twice as long (because he's never done one before). The specialist will charge less than the average lawyer in this type of legal matter because, day in and day out, that's all he does. He can do your work neatly and efficiently in jog time. Locally I have always referred on such matters to *Fulwider, Patton, Reiber, Lee & Utecht* who yellow page-it as "patent attorneys." That's all they do. Their clients range from Walt Disney Productions to the average man in the street. One partner may be handling a case in Oslo, Norway, for Disney while another is back at the office discussing some thingamabob a housewife has just invented. Each client will be charged a reasonable fee. So will you, from any straight-up patent attorney.

Not too many years ago this firm, like other dyed-in-the-wool patent attorneys, could not advertise their specialty. The prospective client—unless he called the bar association—had to grope blindly for a specialist in this field. Now that lawyers are free to advertise the reputable firms will do no more than advise the world that they are "patent attorneys." Francis A. "Pete" Utecht, senior partner in the Fulwider firm, tells me that he now plans to advertise that the patent seeker can "Pro-tect with U-techt." But he says it with a smile on his face and I know he won't. The firm never wants for business!

Criminal law:

This book has made many detrimental remarks about criminal law attorneys but these concerned only those who practice unethically. Even though the numbers of criminal law specialists are increasing, the ethical ones among them are still in the majority.

Almost every law school graduate is so fascinated by the criminal law courses he took (and by what he's seen on TV) that he imagines himself another Clarence Darrow. While, a quarter century ago, it was not too difficult for the average attorney to handle any criminal matter that came along, the criminal law field is today becoming intensely specialized. Appellate or Supreme Court decisions can change the complete complexion of a case overnight. Legislatures seem to be constantly making new laws or altering old ones in this field. To keep abreast of these changes the criminal law specialist must do a lot of reading, attend seminars and keep his eyes and ears open at all times. All he reads, all he hears may have a great effect on cases he now has or may undertake tomorrow.

By the 1980s most state bar associations will allow certification of lawyers plying this trade of Criminal Law Specialist. With such state bar certification you can be assured that these lawyers know their business. Some may play games with you but we trust you will re-read the chapter on Criminal Law before your first appointment!

Workmen's Compensation Law:

Here is a field that requires a steady volume of business to make profits for its practitioners, and the firms specializing in it are usually reliable. Depending, as most do, on referrals from satisfied clients and other attorneys, they will do a good job for the work-injured client. In most instances their fees are set by law and are far lower than their personal injury case brethren might be securing for the same type of (non-job-related) case in the state's regular trial courts. This being so they need to keep their volume high. Shysters will soon fail.

A lawyer in general practice might well be able to handle a workmen's compensation case successfully for you but chances are he'll be sorry he did so. For the work he does times his hourly rate of pay, he'll be grossly underpaid. His specialist friend up the street makes money because he may take two or three compensation cases with him to court every day. My first (and last!) compensation case illustrates what happens. After a period of time I secured an $8,000 award for my client. I felt I had performed $1,500 worth of services. The fee-by-law award was $400. After that I sent my one or two cases a year to a firm in town that did nothing but workmen's compensation. Here again the specialist is your best bet.

Probate:

This Alice-In-Wonderlandlike field has been discussed at length earlier in the book. Although not as grotesque as they were in Charles Dickens's day, probate law and administration are growing more complex with every passing year according to the many probate experts to whom I have talked. Everyone speaks of probate reform but little has been done about it. Perhaps it is just as well. California completely reformed its divorce laws in 1970 and practice under them (which looked easy on paper) has proved far more complex than in the days of the old divorce law. Probate reform, if ever it comes about, would prove little different. Those writing, practicing and judging laws have invariably tried to make them mysterious.

Every city has its probate specialists but only the city's lawyers know who they are. It is certainly hoped that one of the few blessings arising from advertising will be that probate lawyers will announce their specialty to the mystified public. Few will do so at the outset. Only when the advertisers start stealing their business away will they react. At this juncture they will at least announce their specialty in the yellow pages. Bar associations also keep lists of persons who will take referrals in this field but, strangely, many of the better probate lawyers fail to use this avenue to secure more business. Most seem to be satisfied with the practices they have developed—probating the wills they wrote when they were young lawyers.

If you have a court-bound probate matter (some can be disposed of without going to court) by all means seek out the "probate expert." Start with the bar association or friends who have probated estates. Verification through the bar should be made of those who, in the next few years at least, publicly advertise they'll take probate cases. Maybe they will, but are they expert? They may be only games-players who know that probate is a lucrative field of practice.

Be wary of the younger lawyer who claims to be "expert" in this field. Chances are that unless he inherited a bloc of probate cases from his lawyer-father, or is a partner in a strictly-probate firm, he is not what he claims. In twenty-nine years of practice I have had perhaps ten in-court probates. I am by no means an expert in these ritualistic-type proceedings. Seek instead the gray-haired lawyer whose many file cabinets are bulging with wills and probate files. *There's* the lawyer for you.

Taxation:

The certified public accountant is man's best friend in the mad, mad, mad world of taxes. City, county, state and federal taxes, property taxes, income taxes, sales taxes, inheritance taxes. If probate law be called mysterious, tax law is best defined as maddening. Mysterious it can't be called, because with every session of Congress we have tax reform. The tax pauper, driven to frenzy by more and more forms and "enlightened regulations," is driven into the arms of his friendly accountant.

The line between his "accounting advice" and "legal tax advice" is a thin one. A reputable C.P.A. will know the difference. He will refer you to a competent tax lawyer. Should you know your tax problem to involve out-and-out legal work seek only the taxation specialist. The bar association will have a list. Failing this, check with C.P.A.s you know, or whom friends know, for the names of local attorneys who do tax work. Never trust complicated tax matters to an attorney not schooled in this field. One of my late partners specialized in this type of work; he said he spent at least twenty hours a week just reading up on the latest developments in taxation. That was ten years ago. Today he might spend thirty hours a week at the same task.

Beware the lawyer who, in a yellow pages ad, announces that he is a tax expert. Like probate attorneys, real "taxperts" keep their light hidden under a bushel of dignified modesty. I know of at least four really sharp tax attorneys in our city but they are probably known to only one in a thousand laymen.

Many attorneys will handle minimal, routine tax work during the course of, say, a lucrative divorce case or a property-laden probate. The wiser ones will realize when they are getting in over their heads and seek aid from a C.P.A. or tax specialist attorney. Far too many attorneys, however, will let pride stand in their way when it comes to referring matters out. They are struggling in deep water but are too proud to tell their clients they don't know how to swim. Pride goeth before a fall. Should you suspect your attorney is "over his head" either ask out of your contract or ask permission—in tax matters, for example—to see a C.P.A. on your own. As in every legal matter, the money the lawyer is handling belongs to you.

Divorce:

Any lawyer *should* be able to handle a simple, uncontested divorce. "Divorce Clinics" run by laymen who supply forms, typing and directions to the courthouse also successfully handle the simplest of these cases. A rule of thumb, however, should be this: if your divorce has the possibility of being contested and if it involves alimony, child support or extensive money/property holdings, by all means retain an attorney. Even so, the pathway from his office to the final decree of divorce is fraught with many perils. All or any of these items are important to you: child support, alimony, property and money. There are many ways to lose them and once lost they can never be regained. Do not, to save a few dollars in fees, run your own divorce through where these issues are involved. Many do so only to find out later, sometimes years later, that the divorce decree was faultily drawn up and cannot be enforced. A do-it-yourselfer is putty in the hands of a divorce lawyer expert handling the case for the oppsoing spouse.

Divorce lawyers who will play games with you have been discussed earlier. Watch for these games at all times. It is my own opinion that the percentage of unethical lawyers confining themselves to divorce law is rising more rapidly than the percentage of their confreres in any other legal field.

Advertising will bring out so-called divorce specialists even before lawyers in other fields have had time to prepare their ads. I say "so-called" because the real specialists will remain buried in the yellow pages or in bar association lists. These *real* specialists are the guys and gals you'll want to handle your divorce.

Bankruptcy:

Back in 1950 I became friends with a young Los Angeles attorney named Houston Slate. Like myself, Hugh was fielding whatever cases were coming along and waiting for the "big break." Those who get such breaks usually make them on their own, which is what Hugh did. Having handled a few bankruptcies, and enjoyed the work, he spread the word among other lawyers that he would be glad to take their bankruptcy referrals. Now if there is one case that requires a lot of time for a small reward (if the lawyer charges reasonably), it is the bankruptcy. This, added to the fact that clients often do not pay their full fee in these cases, leads many lawyers to avoid them. On the average every lawyer will get at least one or two calls each year to handle bankruptcies. Luckily for Hugh the other lawyers cooperated in his plan. By working long hours, seven days a week, Hugh was able to tackle successfully the voluminous paperwork involved in every bankruptcy, and shepherd his clients through the nearby bankruptcy courts. Soon afterwards he partnered with young, go-getting attorney Andy Leoni and the firm of Slate & Leoni was on its way. Handling nothing but matters arising under the federal bankruptcy laws, they grew to be the number one firm in that field in the state of California. Though most of their cases are still referred to them by other attorneys, satisfied clients send in a good share every year. A general practitioner handling a bankruptcy would be likely to spend far more time on it, and thus charge far more for it, than would Slate & Leoni. Many dozens of secretaries, a competent staff of attorneys and a growing number of branch offices allow them to do more work, more cheaply, and more quickly than could the average, nonspecialist lawyer.

Unless yours is the simplest of no-asset bankruptcies which any young lawyer could and would like to handle, it is best that you retain the specialist. Call them for quotes on fees; call other lawyers, compare prices. Invariably the specialist will be charging less. As the outcome of this kind of case is of the utmost importance to the client, he should be certain there are no slip-ups, no faulty orders, no failure to list proper debts and assets. A specialist will make certain.

"Bankruptcy Clinics," run by laymen are also coming into vogue in the larger cities. They will provide forms for you. You complete them in longhand and they type them up. You are given directions to the courthouse and information (never *legal advice* per se) on what to do when Bankruptcy Day arrives, as a person can be his or her own attorney in bankruptcy matters, and a growing number are. In the simplest cases, with or without the help of lay clinics, the average person should be able to handle his or her own case. Before doing anything, however, compare prices. For a few dollars more you might be able to secure the services of a lawyer-expert. It would be worth it.

The basic game lawyers play in bankruptcies is

overcharging. The unethical lawyer will either spend more hours on a case than it strictly requires, or increase his normal hourly fee. With no bar association minimum fee guidelines for him to follow (see chapter 12, "What *Is* Your Fee?"), he sets the sky as his limit—if he can get it! By simply calling a bankruptcy-specialist friend, however, he can learn what the going rate is.

A referee in bankruptcy may also decide to cut down the fee a lawyer has charged you. If, after such a decision, the attorney fails to refund the balance due to you, or asks for extra money "under the table" he is acting unethically. He is playing games with you. Don't let him get away with it.

Personal injury litigation:

There are as many types of personal injury suits as there are ways for people to become injured. One—workmen's compensation—has already been discussed. The vast majority of the others fall into three main categories:

(1) auto accidents,
(2) product liability matters and
(3) slip and fall accidents.

Those who earn the most money in these fields are the specialists. They are the ones who can get you "top dollar" for your injury if there are dollars to be gotten for the case at all (some, don't forget, *are* losers). These specialists are the ones who, year in and year out, get to know and understand the insurance adjusters, judges and juries with whom they must deal. They become as familiar with every facet of their work as the brain surgeon becomes expert on every crevice of the brain. Seeking the highest possible settlement or award for their clients they do not hustle a case through in jig-time just for the sake of a quick buck.

The "hustlers" are the games-players in this field.

Watch out for them. They work on a volume basis and, as was discussed in the Personal Injury chapter, make fast dollars for themselves but fewer than they could have for you. Also be wary of the novice attorney who will take a complicated, big money case and not seek outside help. His pride is false, and you may well be hurt by the results of his amateur efforts.

Personal injury cases can result in some giant settlements and mammoth jury awards. The attorney, generally working on a percentage basis, makes a good fee. This gold that glitters in the personal injury hills attracts many lawyers, especially the young ones with high overheads and low incomes. Advertisements by lawyers seeking personal injury work will become popular in the months and years ahead—be wary of these guys too. The topflight specialists won't advertise. Call your bar association for their names. Since their fees will undoubtedly be on a percentage basis you stand to get more for your money with a pro than with an amatuer. Lawyer A may get you $100,000 for your case; he takes a third as his fee. Lawyer B, charging the same third, might only have been able to squeeze $50,000 from the insurance carrier or jury. Be practical. Secure the services of the expert.

Admirality:

Here is a specialty so rare that it is only in larger seaport cities that you find its practitioners. Few lawyers dare walk through its maze of strange laws and odd-sounding rules and regulations. Those who have legal matters arising in this category should by all means secure the services of the firm legitimately holding itself out to be admiralty specialists. If your area has no such bird have a local attorney consult Martindale-Hubbell, the leading national attorneys' directory. Checking the biographical pages of seaport city attorneys (e.g. Long Beach, San Francisco and Seattle on the West Coast) you should be able to find competent counsel.

Bona fide admiralty lawyers rarely play games. They are proud of their unique field of law and of their specialization in it. A good rapport between the relatively few admiralty attorneys in the United States (and around the world) is a *must* in this business. A shyster wouldn't last very long with these boys. Found out for what he was, he'd be drummed out of the corps.

Our town is blessed with having the state's leading admiralty firm, *Ackerman, Ling & Russell.* I envy them the trips on which their admiralty adventures take them—Hong Kong, Rio, Honolulu and the far-flung ports of the world. Ah, to realize too late that I should have asked Jim Ackerman for a job when I was a young lawyer! I sent Jim the only admiralty matter that ever wandered through my doors. It was a small case but he let me accompany him on the trip it involved—a drive twenty-five miles up the road to Los Angeles.

Young lawyers

Yes, the young lawyer is a specialist in his own right. He specializes in vim and vigor—the ability to work long into the night and through weekends. The older lawyers look upon him with envy (nostalgia?) as he races around the courthouse on any given day covering four separate court calendars on three different floors. They silently cheer him as he makes the fourth calendar-call in the nick of time, out of breath but ready to go. Maury Wills sliding home with the winning run.

The younger lawyer specializes in time; he has a lot of it to give you. Recalling my first divorce case, mentioned earlier, the reader remembers I was able to devote an entire month to it. No case since; divorce or otherwise, has had so much straight, uninterrupted time spent on it. So it may be that your case is the only one your young lawyer has at the moment. What he lacks in experience can be made up for in large part by research and action.

Of course there are good guys and bad guys among the younger set as among the older. The problem with the former is that the bad guys have not surfaced yet. Who can tell, looking at them all in a row as they are sworn in as lawyers, which are out to make a fast buck at anyone's expense, which are the ethical ones? Which ones in the latter group will succumb to avarice, greed and dishonesty during their careers? Who among the fast-buck artists will reform? Such are the questions the prospective client must ask when facing the obviously "new" lawyer. He may be getting another Abraham Lincoln but at the same time the young man might be an admirer of the convicted Watergate lawyers.

Once the case is under way you, as an observant client, can more readily spot the games your young lawyer may be playing than you would if he were an older lawyer. The new lawyer, inexperienced in games-playing-for-real, may be clumsy and obvious in his attempts to fool you. At this stage you can warn him that you are on to his game, or simply leave and seek services elsewhere. The older lawyer, more experienced in games-playing will be an old smoothie; you may never know what happened.

The odds are that more young lawyers are on the take today than was the case a generation ago or before that. The mighty influx of new lawyers swamping the land will be the cause. This is not to say that older lawyers are necessarily clean. Some have been unethical since their first days of practice; more than a few others have turned to games-playing because of (a) the pinch of inflation and (b) the upsurge in competition.

It is hoped that this book will not become a primer for young lawyers wanting to play games on an unsuspecting public. You, having read the book, however, will be on to these games. Hopefully you will know when they are being played. The best a novice, first-year, lawyer can do is play them clumsily.

The old and the young in law are as the young and old in life itself. We look at the youngster and wish we had his vitality; it is only sad he doesn't have our experience. The youngster in turn scorns our weariness but secretly longs for the day when he, too, will have experience. You can't have both in the law business!

The law is replete with other specialties. Should you become involved in one that is not mentioned here, be advised that the games discussed in this book are found in every legal field. Keep a weather eye open. If, by case's end, you find that all has gone well then you can be sure you had as your lawyer one of an endangered species—the ethical attorney.

CHAPTER 19

Games Lawyers Play on Each Other

During my first year of practice I had an office on the edge of town. As is true with many young lawyers who come to the Big City cold-turkey and unknown, I almost starved. I met few other lawyers. At year's end I was saved from oblivion by a downtown lawyer who took me into his office at a cheap rent and gave me a goodly number of referrals from his overcrowded desk.

One of the first things this older lawyer (Big John) did was take me aside and tell me who the three "shysters" were in our city. Three! Three lawyers he said could never be trusted and with whom I should always deal with extreme caution. Over the years I met all of them on the opposite side of cases. Two tried to give me the trouble John had predicted, the third proved to be one of the good guys. Perhaps he had reformed in his old age.

In any event, what John was trying to point out, and what I learned from experience, is that any lawyer can do a better job for his clients if he establishes good relationships with other attorneys. During the running of a case we must take the opposing lawyer's word for many things. We must often act on his oral agreement, believe him when he shakes hands on a settlement. If he tells us he will produce a witness at trial who will testify to facts A, B and C we will believe him and plan our case accordingly. If we are on a week's vacation, or a month's, we will not worry about our lawyer friends knifing our case in the back during our absence. They too will be taking vacations. If one refuses to allow us to postpone a case for a legitimate reason, forcing us to court to get a court order, he can expect the same treatment should he suddenly need a postponement. The base of our operations as lawyers depends in large part on our trust in and friendships with other lawyers in the community. In the background lies the fear of retaliation should we get out of line and start drifting toward a shyster existence.

The games-playing lawyer will hurt your case because word will have spread quickly through the legal community that we have another shyster in our midst. Beware! This lawyer will be required to do far more work on your case than he would if he were a man to be trusted. Many things the opposing lawyer might allow him if he were to be trusted, he must now go to court to secure. Other lawyers won't take *his* word for anything, so he must constantly correspond, "to verify in writing what I told you on the phone today." The ethical lawyer can, quite legitimately, spring giant surprises on the shyster in the courtroom.

In one of my earlier cases I had the wife in a divorce case. Everything was going my way and I was sure we would make out well in court. The other lawyer, strangely, made no offer of settlement. Three days before we were to go to court I got a call from him.

"I just can't do it to you," he said. "You're too nice a guy."

"Do what to me when?" I asked, flattered at being considered a nice guy.

It turned out that, quite unbeknownst to me, my client had been fooling around with half a dozen different lovers, writing letters to them and sending them keys to her back door. Unfortunately the parties' under-age children lived with her and her sort of conduct was strictly verboten in those days. The husband would win their custody (and possession of the home and have to make no alimony payments) because of his wife's amorous adventures. My opponent could have sprung this on me in court. There was no requirement that he tell me. Had we gone to court he could have used the evidence but at least I would have been well forewarned. As it was the client quickly became reconciled with her husband when I phoned her the news.

"I wish it had been X on the other side of this case instead of you," the other lawyer later told me, naming one of the town's then three shysters. "I'd have loved to have shot him down in the courtroom."

Cooperation from opposing attorneys can save a client many dollars during the course of an average case. Friendship begets trust and this, in turn, is the very basis on which the lawyer versus lawyer system operates.

Today's lawyers either aren't learning this or are forgetting it. I have seen and heard about more back-stabbing among lawyers in the last few years than in all my previous years combined. It is getting so one doesn't know who to trust these days.

A friend of mine told me that he recently was required to leave town unexpectedly during a week in which a small case was due for trial. The other lawyer, whom he had no reason not to trust, readily agreed to appear in court on the date set and secure a short continuance, no problem. When my friend returned he found that his opponent had gone to court all right but had taken a default judgment against him. He was forced to go to court to have it set aside (easily set aside when the judge heard what had happened). There went one name from his list of guys and gals he could trust.

I had several hefty stabs in my back in the year prior to my last heart attack and subsequent Farewell to Divorce. One was from a young man to whom, when he was new in town, I'd given much creditable publicity while writing for our local lawyers magazine; I even sent him a case from time to time. When he pulled a fast one on me I couldn't believe it. "Who can one trust these days?" I asked myself.

Though he snidely smiles at the successful games he plays on other lawyers, the shyster fails to realize that the word spreads quickly along the legal grapevine. Sooner or later his tricks will catch up with him. No lawyer will take his word for anything and his work will be doubled and his income slip because of it.

Every mistake he may make in every case will be capitalized upon by his opposition. Why not? Law is an adversary proceeding and as long as one acts ethically, fair is fair.

What may hurt your games-playing lawyer even more—and ultimately hurt you—is the fact the judges, too, soon get the word on who are the good guys, who are the bad. Time after time over the years I have seen situations arise where a judge was required to take or reject a lawyer's word for something.

"My client is at home ill," the lawyer advises the court, "I verified it with his doctor just this morning."

How does the judge know? If the lawyer is known to be a congenital liar the court may not grant the continuance (postponement) he seeks.

"In the Supreme Court case of Fleegel versus Beegel," says the lawyer, giving the exact case citation, "the court ruled so and so."

Should the judge hold this lawyer's ethics in high regard he will take his word that Fleegel versus Beegel contained this language. If the shyster made the same quote the judge might take a few minutes to retire to his chambers to check on the Fleegel decision.

When the final, decision-making task is upon him the judge must weigh the evidence presented by both parties. While the ethical lawyer's witnesses may have been lying, the judge concludes there was no chance they were coached to do so. The odds that they were telling the truth are better than the odds that the opposing witnesses were doing so. After all, their disreputable attorney may have coached them to tell the truth as he, the attorney, wanted it to be. Not all cases, of course, are decided by one lawyer's reputation being set against another's. Enough of them are, however, to possibly hurt you if you are the games-playing attorney's client in this case.

Beware then, not only the games a shyster may play on you, but also the games he may propose to play on the other party's counsel. Since you may well hate the other party (your wife or husband, for example), you may get a momentary thrill in knowing your mouth-piece is going to play some tricks on his counterpart. Let the thrill be only momentary. In the end, if enough of these tricks are pulled, the opponent may be saving one final Big Surprise for you. If it is saved for use at the appropriate time in the courtroom, you lose. What good then are the tricks your lawyer pulled along the way? And, if he was dirty-pooling the opposition all the while, might he not have been playing secret games with your money along the way?

Steer clear of the braggart. Good lawyers don't need to brag about their victories, honest ones never do. The lawyer who tells you he never lost a case is either lying or has had a mighty short career. The big boys in the business, the Bellis, Baileys, Lincolns and Darrows, were oft-time losers. Unfortunately, the news media always played up their wins, never mentioned their losses. The myth that really good lawyers never lose cases is just that, a myth. Should the lawyer you have selected use the bragging routine during your first visit, bid him adieu. His game is your loss. His fellow attorneys also dislike him and stay clear of him at cocktail parties or bar association functions. They know him as more bull than brains. Judges doze while he is talking, juries sleep.

The "mirror, mirror on the wall, who's the richest of us all" game is played *with* fellow attorneys for social reasons, *on* clients for economic gain.

Social life in lawyering society is not an easy go. Popular opinion to the contrary, there are some very wealthy lawyers but just as many low-income ones, while most are clambering up and down the ladder in between. It has always seemed to me that the medical community in any city is more stable financially than its lawyers. The latter have learned, however, that "the appearance of wealth" is just as important as wealth itself. The observations that you and I make along life's way show why, for if a person appears wealthy we assume that he is. It is only after we come into close daily contact with people, or are their bankers, that we know, or *may* know, the true condition of their wealth.

I knew two lawyers very well for almost twenty years prior to their untimely deaths from heart attacks when they were in their late forties. Both died of overwork. Both, year after year, earned the same income. Yet one had yachts, big homes, high-fashion clothing and the best of everything; the other lived modestly. The first claimed wise investments accounted for his wealth; the second lived as comfortably as an old shoe and with no display of ostentation. When their estates were finally probated it was found that the "rich guy" was a million dollars in debt; he had wheeled and dealed his way to apparent wealth. His counterpart died even on the books—a few debts, a few assets and no insurance (he'd "never had time" to take the requisite medical exams!). Probably without realizing it, many of you know lawyers of the first type.

A position of wealth is important to most lawyers because they "run" together, at social events, bar functions, club meetings, and in their day-to-day courthouse dealings. Any class of persons, thrown into such intimate and enduring association, will be easily corrupted by the sin of envy, and many lawyers are so corrupted. They see an old law school buddy driving a big Caddy and living in the best section of town. Envy creeps in. Few will ask if the Caddy and home are mortgaged to the hilt, and the "rich guy" won't tell. Lawyers' wives play a great part in the apparent-wealth-game too. Thrown together at soirées or bridge parties they soon notice that lawyers A and B are living high on the hog, and ask, why can't we?

"Well," you answer, "lawyer A inherited his money and lawyer B inherited his. I married a poor but beautiful girl."

"How about C and D," the wife presses on, not noticing the flattery.

Lawyer C has you stumped. You have always wondered how he can live so well. Lawyer D, you are forced to admit, has been successful in his practice.

Many lawyers, yielding to social pressure, will buy bigger homes and better homes than they can afford. They will become expert practitioners of the credit card game. Legally "padding" financial statements for bank loans will come easy to them. Like my old friend lawyer Number One they, too, will soon be a million or more in hock. So long as they stay alive they can wheel and deal and do it. Such persons, and there is a growing number of them, can now keep up with the Jones and enjoy the Good Life. The only thing missing is peace of mind.

The game of trying to keep up with each other economically (and therefore socially) trickles over into these lawyers' business lives. If their apparent wealth is a million, for example, and it takes a $100,000 a year income to live that way (which it does), and if they are only earning $50,000 a year when the game begins, they must increase their income in some manner. The games you have read about in this book provide the means of accomplishing this end. Guess who pays for "apparent wealth?" You do!

Games within games. One is to impress your client with wealth; this spells success. Another is to impress your client that you are just as he is, poor but honest. In the larger metropolitan areas, particularly on the West Coast, clients seem to be impressed by the lavish decor of their lawyers' offices. Plush offices spell wealth and this in turn must mean that the lawyer is successful. Ability being the handmaiden of success, this then is the lawyer for them. They rarely guess who is paying for all of these fine trappings. Few know that the lawyers down the street in the modest clinic are just as good as their newly-found mouthpiece and charge half the price.

The phenomenon of the plush West Coast lawyer is due in large part to the steady influx of outsiders into the area. Having little else to measure success by, these cling to the age-old belief that the appearance of wealth and success are one and the same. The concept of the old family lawyer never became fully rooted in California, as it did in the East and the Midwest.

Even within one area in California some new offices will appear luxurious and others quite modest. As a child I was always impressed with the law office next door to my father's. It had deep-pile carpeting, rich drapes and an aura of elegance. Dad's was a rather barren affair, clean and neat but devoid of trappings. Only when I was older did I realize why all this was so. The lawyer in the swanky office had corporate offices, bankers and business executives as clients; they expected classy surroundings. Father's clients, on the other hand, were primarily the Norwegian farmers of the county. They wanted to see *him,* not be impressed with a swanky office.

"If I dolled up my office like X has [naming his next door lawyer-neighbor]," Dad said, "I wouldn't have a client left in a week. They'd think I was putting on airs and they're wise enough to know who'd be paying for it."

"But you can speak Norwegian to them," I persisted, "and you grew up on a farm like they did."

"There are a dozen lawyers in town who could say the same," he answered.

Discussion closed.

The Paramount/Artesia area of southern California was once a rich farm belt. It still is to a great extent, but many a cow pasture is now a housing tract. I know some very wealthy lawyers up there and all have modest offices. Their farmer-clients, rich or poor, want a thrifty lawyer. Ten miles away, right on the beach, are some of America's most luxurious law offices.

During my law school days in Texas some decades ago, I found that lawyers had two public images insofar as the appearances they kept. During the business day they would dress in unpretentious clothing and drive old cars; their offices were neat but far from glamorous. In the evening they would drive home to their mansions-on-the-hill, change into white tie and tails and go to formal dinners in their hidden Cadillacs (Lincolns and foreign cars were not "in" cars in those days). The young man sitting next to me in many of my law school classes was the object of my sympathy for a year or more; he dressed in old clothes and drove a battered wreck of a car to school. He seemed just a plain country boy working his way through law school. Only in my final year did I find out his family was among the wealthiest in the state. On the other hand the richly-dressed man sitting opposite me was forced to drop out of law school because of a lack of funds. *He* was the poor boy. As I found out in Texas, you can't always tell by appearances. Texans judge a man by what he is, not by the razzle-dazzle he can generate.

Lawyers' homes, autos, clothing and accoutrements are a part of their family overhead; their offices—from law books to interior decoration—reflect the expense of their office overheads. Each overhead must be paid for in some manner. Clients pay for it. As office overheads alone absorb around 40 percent of a lawyer's gross income, you can pretty well tell from the decor of his office, and the size of his library, what all of it is costing him. The attorney who must pay out or depreciate $1000 per month for his office will necessarily need more, and be charging more, than the lawyer who gets by on $500 a month. Look around the office when visiting a lawyer for the first time. Is it a miniature Taj Mahal? Does his library rival the nearby county law library in size? If so you can figure on contributing to its upkeep when it comes time to pay your fee. If you don't mind spending extra money so that you too can luxuriate in these swank surroundings for a while, fine. Perhaps a corporation, your mother or Uncle Sam is picking up the tab. If it isn't *your* money you might as well follow the Federal Rule: spend it, there's always more where that came from.

Burdened by inflation and increasing competition, however, more and more lawyers are learning that the public, faced itself with austerity, will not let its selection of an attorney be governed by the decoration of his office. The increasing popularity of law clinics attest to this fact. Attorneys are likewise finding that the spiraling cost of maintaining a large library can be eliminated by visiting a nearby county or bar association library. It's becoming standard practice for most lawyers to have the basic set of laws of their own state, plus a small selection of books within the field of their specialty. Don't look for a gigantic library except in the largest of law offices. The chances are that a solo lawyer with a fancy spread of books has not even touched, much less opened, 90 percent of them. There's no need for you to pay for this touch of class that he's added to his overhead.

On your first visit to a previously unknown lawyer, inquire as to his local bar association ties. Is he a member? Has he served it as an officer, a member of the board, or in some other capacity? If his answers are in the affirmative you have some assurance that he is held in high regard by his fellow attorneys. Games-playing attorneys aren't, although it must be admitted a few do work their way into the heart of a bar association from time to time. The man well thought of by his fellow attorneys won't play games with them, nor they with him. This small but important factor will, in the long run, prove to be a great aid in the successful handling of your case.

Lawyers, unfortunately, will continue to play more and more games with each other. This in turn will lead to more and more games being played with *you*. Lawyers seem uninterested in stopping this trend (or are they unable to stop it?). You alone can do it by nipping their games in the bud.

CHAPTER 20

Games of the Future

There are probably other games being played today by ne'er-do-well attorneys which I have failed to outline. This is not neglect on my part but simply that I haven't heard about them as yet. If there is one thing an attorney learns from experience, it is that the longer he practices the less he seems to know about the law. The only time a lawyer can lay claim to knowing everything is the day he passes his Bar exams and begins practice. In his first case he will find out something he didn't know before. The experience will be good for him, for in the next case he can profit by it. The trouble is that in the next case he also learns something new. The chain is endless and after 3,000 cases you know that every case is alike and yet every case is different. So, too, not ever having practiced in certain fields, I may not have reported on games being played there. The bigger games, prevalent in all fields of practice, have been the ones spotlighted in this book.

What of the future? Lawyers have ingenious minds. They are forever coming up with new ideas, new slants on old ideas, new ways of doing things. So it is that men who each day carefully plan trial strategy, weigh evidence, give brilliant speeches, and are right now concocting advertising campaigns, should have no trouble figuring out new games to play.

You just cannot take the 500,000 lawyers who will be in practice in America by the end of the year 1977 and not find some thousands of them who will not stoop to unethical practice, who will not play games on their clients. A mere 10 percent of these lawyers adds up to 50,000. If these are split equally between the states that makes 1,000 per state. Of course, California and New York, with their disproportionate number of lawyers will have a disproportionate number of unethical ones. But the situation is likely to get worse: the fiercer the competition, the lower the ethics. If unscrupulous lawyers of the near future have a tough time embezzling (because there's little money to embezzle) and zeroing in on back accounts (because what few clients they have are poverty-stricken), their ingenious minds will surely find other games to play.

False advertising is one—pretending to be a specialist in a certain legal field when you are not. There may be new twists in the ambulance-chasing racket, e.g., planting *paid* runners/cappers in large offices, as regular employees of those offices, to encourage litigation among fellow employees. A criminal client, specializing in burglaries may find an attorney willing to aid him in the planning and later cover-up in a series of "burgs," all in return for a "cut of the swat." It's happened often enough on TV and in the flicks!

Forgery, now rarely dabbled in by attorneys for fear of both bar association and criminal court consequences, may become an oft-played game. Checks, drafts and other negotiable instruments, together with deeds and commercial papers often come across a lawyer's desk. Lawyer-forgeries of such papers have been reported in the past so we know that the game has been invented. Will the pressure of hard times encourage lawyers to play it more often?

And what of new fields of law that haven't even come into being as yet? Divorce, for example, was said to have been "invented" by Henry VIII. It wasn't, of course, but divorce suits were exceedingly rare until the 20th century. The games that some lawyers play in divorce cases are inventions of the last 75–100 years. If there were no divorces and no criminal cases today, the courts would be hard pressed for business.

Personal injury suits arising from auto accidents became really big time only after World War II. In that post-war era liability insurance for automobiles became compulsory in most states. An ever-increasing number of auto accident personal injury cases flooded the courts. Games involving this type of suit came into being.

Who knows how many new fields of law may open up in the future? But when new fields do come along you can bet your bottom dollar that there will be lawyer games accompanying.

What you can do about games of the future

Continue, from now until doomsday, to secure the services of an attorney through solid, reputable sources—bar associations, friends who have been "satisfied customers," the referrals of competent lawyers. Third-hand recommendations are no good at all. That a friend of a friend of a friend of yours knows a "really neat lawyer" is not a recommendation; "neat" may mean looks and personality, not legal ability. Many very good lawyers would win "Mr. Ugly" contests!

Keep a wary eye on the games that your lawyer may be playing on you. Keep close tabs on your case at all times. Count the money coming in and make sure it's safe in a bank rather than being toted to the racetrack by your friendly ("real neat") attorney. I continue to be amazed at people who seem to forget their cases once they've started them: the heirs who waited eight years before blowing the whistle on their probate attorney, the lady who did not question her attorney's failure to give her a settlement for two and a half years—these have been mentioned and similar cases may be read about in any newspaper. Those that never reach the ears of a newspaper reporter are legion.

Remain on good terms with your attorney. Solid rapport is always a must in the attorney/client relationship and cannot be overemphasized. Be wary of overfriendliness on his part, however; he may want you as a playing partner instead of a client.

The future also holds the possibility of another

deadly game. Unlike the games delineated earlier in this book, this game is one which lawyers are beginning to play on themselves. Someday, if the game continues at its present pace, there may be no lawyers at all!

The gambit is the use and hiring by lawyers of legal assistants or, as they are often called, *para-legals*. These people are not lawyers. They are employed by attorneys to do research, prepare pleadings and, often, to interview clients. Most are in law school but this is not a requirement. They can do almost everything except go to court and sign their names to legal documents. Those I have met and of whom I have heard do competent jobs. You are paying for them, of course, for their salaries are included in office overheads and this is passed on to you through the hourly fees your attorney charges. The client hires the lawyer but nonlawyers do much of the work.

Another nonlawyer working for the client is the legal secretary. A competent one is worth her weight in gold. Many a probate attorney depends almost entirely on a trained probate secretary to grind out on her own the many pleadings, papers, accountings and reports necessary to run a probate through from beginning to end. She often interviews clients as well— something most experienced legal secretaries find easy to do. You pay *her* salary through your fees.

The game, then, is one in which you pay a good-sized hourly fee to the attorney but only a small portion of it is paid back to his secretary or para-legals, or both; on the other hand these employees are performing a good 50 percent of the time charged for in your case. The game is also a trap for lawyers. Slowly but surely they are depending more and more on nonlawyer help for their offices—from para-legals, law clerks and well-trained legal secretaries. The latter in turn are demanding (and rightly) higher wages each year to meet cost-of-living increases. The lawyer must eventually find himself unable to increase his hourly fees to you because, down the street, a cut-rate lawyer is enticing so much new business through his neon-framed doors. The overabundance of new lawyers will put a ceiling on what all lawyers will be able to charge. As their basic overheads keep on increasing their net profits will start declining. Will it then come to a battle of the lawyers versus the nonlawyers in the field of lawyering?

The answer to this question may lie in a problem that has faced two-year junior colleges in California and elsewhere in the nation these past several years. Many such colleges have extensive evening programs. The teachers for these classes are paid on an hourly basis, whereas daytime teachers are hired on a regular yearly contract at a set sum. Not too many years ago one bright evening teacher divided the number of hours a daytime teacher taught into the total amount he earned and was aghast to find that the daytimers were earning almost twice as much as the evening instructors. One thing led to another and soon there was tremendous pressure on junior college school districts to bring nighttimers *up* to parity with the daytimers. (Never was it suggested that the contract teachers' salaries be lowered so as to equal hourly teachers pay!) Suits were filed, petitions brought, unions formed. "More pay, or bust!" was the slogan.

"Bust" will probably be the answer. Teaching evenings myself, and knowing the financial situation of most school districts, I suspected it would bankrupt even the affluent districts should they put hourly and contract instructors on a parity. I voiced my opinion to a long-time friend, a member of a district education board, and was assured I was right. He thought the problem could be resolved.

The problem is being resolved. Many districts are now beginning to hire regular contract teachers on the basis of their being required to teach at least one evening class under their contracts. Once this program gets underway the hourly nighttime educator will be slowly phased out. Not too many years from now "hourlies" will cease to exist. They wanted more but will end up getting nothing.

There will also be a fade-out of a class within the field of lawyering. The daytime/nighttime teacher situation will be played out in reverse. Lawyers may well disappear as a segment of our society. Since nonlawyers are doing so much legal work now, the public will soon wonder why they can't do *all* of this work. Why not phase out your $75 an hour lawyer for a $20 an hour para-legal?

Things are already moving in that direction. Throughout the country divorce and bankruptcy "clinics" are increasing in number. A sampling from a daily metropolitan newspaper reveals a few of the classified ads which advertise these services:

These are the non-law-office laymen at work. There is nothing illegal about providing you with proper forms, typing them for you and then telling you where to file them. Theoretically no legal advice is given by the clinic worker. State bar associations have been fighting these clinics for years but they continue to flourish.

Soon para-legals, law clerks and legal secretaries, thwarted in their efforts to get pay raises each year, will move out of the law office onto the street. They will set up their own clinics. With their background and training they will provide better service than most such clinics and councils do today. The public, ever looking for a bargain, will follow them.

Lurking in the background is a bogeyman that lawyers have feared since the birth of their profession— the fact that a person may not need a lawyer to represent him in court. He can be his own attorney.

As nonlawyers proliferate in the field of law, lawyers may well find themselves being phased out neatly and quietly and as surely as the nighttime teachers who dared ask for more. If present trends continue the system as we now know it may well cease to exist.

The formula is a simple one: too many lawyers leads to a deterioration of ethics. This cancer in turn weakens the entire profession. It becomes sickly. Soon you, the court-bound litigant, will by-pass the lawyer for the nonlawyer. His fees are too high and you're not at all certain of his ethics. The nonlawyer, on the other hand, charges much less, and how can he get unethical handing you forms, filling them out for you and telling you what to do with them? Lawyering dies. The games have ended.

* * *

Life, of course, is always changing. Should lawyering die, the prices charged by nonlawyer clinics will go up. No longer competing with lawyers, the former para-legal or legal secretary will be able to charge more. Costs to the layman will probably reflect that old familiar "whatever the traffic will bear" philosophy. A new and increasingly affluent class will arise—the nonlawyer legal helper.

GETTUS & WEAP
N.L.L.H.
We'll take everyone and anything.
We do the paperwork—you go to court.

The tide sweeps shoreward. Lawyers, scrambling in the sea of wide-open advertising and scrambling for a buck, don't see it. If, too late, they are washed ashore, their profession may forever lay stranded on the beach. Too late then to stop playing games and pay attention to the business of ethics.

BE YOUR OWN LAWYER the frequent ads of the *Citizens Legal Protective League* tell us. This national organization, based in Sanford, Florida, may be telling us what the future holds. If games are then being played, you'll be playing them on yourselves!

* * *

Finally, don't send *me* any legal business as a result of your reading this book. After two heart attacks (both of which my doctors attribute to my law practice) and having lost two law partners (ages 45 and 48) to heart attacks, I've decided it's time to sit on the sidelines and, from a distance and with better perspective, *write* about the practice of law rather than be involved in it. I hope I can do it. The wear and tear is too great and I would rather live to romp with what I hope will be many grandchildren than die in the quest for the Almighty Dollar.

Clients play games with lawyers too. Older lawyers, cynical and hard-bitten by years of practice, can recognize these games and brush them aside. Many are the starry-eyed younger lawyers, however, who have ridden into the field of law on a white horse looking for "Justice." With these young men (and some of the older ones who have valiantly kept such naivete alive in their bosoms) the public can play its own games. But, then, this is a story for another book.

FINAL CHECK-LIST TO BE READ BEFORE VISITING A LAWYER

1. If your case falls within the scope of cases discussed in this book, review those chapters or passages again. Be ready!

2. Did you select your lawyer through proper channels? If you secured his name through the bar association or a friend who was satisfied with his services and recommended him, the chances are better that he will be ethical.

3. If you were unable to secure a bar association or satisfied-friend recommendation to the lawyer you have chosen, be sure to ask *him* a few questions before you start your case interview. How long has he been in practice? (check his law school and state bar plaques on the wall). Is he experienced in the type of case you have? (if so, have him outline a few of his more successful results). Talk to him awhile. Get the "feel" for the kind of guy he is, or isn't.

4. Review the facts of your case again. Make certain you have everything down "pat" this time so a second conference won't be necessary to fill him in on things you forgot to tell him the first time around. Since lawyers sell Time you'll be paying for your forgetfulness.

5. If you have physical evidence—account books, pictures, letters and the like—make certain you bring these along. Any of these may turn into "proof" in

court and a good lawyer cannot take your word that such items exist unless he has them in hand.

6. If your case concerns a particular writing—deed, letter, contract—be certain you bring this along. The lawyer must see it since the heart of your case rests on the exact wording in the document in question. (So many people stop to ask me about a deed or contract they signed but, not being able to see it, I cannot advise them. What they believe the writing said and what it really says in legal terms, may be two different things!)

7. If you are going to a lawyer who advertised his prices, take the ad along. When he then tells you his fee will be higher than quoted, you can argue the point with him or, better yet, leave the office. Few are the towns that have but one lawyer.

8. Dress modestly. Most lawyers still believe that people who "dude up", wear diamonds and "act rich", are rich. They can set their fees accordingly. Come straight from your job in work clothes. The good lawyer will admire you for not getting "duded-up", as they say in Texas.

9. Ree-lax! The unethical lawyer can take advantage of the up-tight, nervous and often frightened client. The relaxed client can more easily notice games, if games it is his lawyer would play with him; he can avert these games because he is in control of his mind.

10. Arrive at the office a few minutes early, never late. Call in advance if you must cancel or postpone the appointment. Courtesy offered may be courtesy repaid later.

Bar Associations

Local (City or County) Bar Associations:

The local bar association is your best bet for *finding an attorney*. Most have reference services which categorize lawyers by their specialties. State bar associations, as a rule, do not carry such referral lists. Referrals from local associations are not foolproof but your chances of getting a competent attorney are far better when selected through this system as opposed to blindly choosing a lawyer with no recommendation.

Local associations are listed in the telephone directory white pages and, in increasing numbers, in the yellow pages under "Attorneys." Many associations carry small ads in the yellow pages as well. They are as interested in your securing the services of a competent attorney as you are.

State Bar Associations:

State associations should be contacted for serious complaints you have against an attorney. They, *not* the local associations, have the supreme disciplinary power—suspension or disbarment from practice—over attorneys.

Local associations can censure an attorney for unethical conduct but this does not prevent his continuing it. Of course one action they can take is to strike a lawyer's name from their referral lists. As lawyers are becoming more and more dependent on these referrals for a source of income, this may deter them from playing games. Only your complaints to the bar association, however, can achieve this end. Unless they hear from *you* they may never know that this lawyer or that is playing games.

The following is the 1977 list of state bar associations:

Directory of Bar Associations

STATE BAR ASSOCIATIONS

Association	Write or Phone:
	Executive Director or Executive Secretary
*Alabama State Bar	Reginald T. Hamner P. O. Box 671 Montgomery 36101 205/269-1515
Alaska Bar Assn.	Mary F. LaFollette Box 279 Anchorage 99501 907/272-7469
State Bar of Arizona	Eldon L. Husted Ste. 858 234 N. Central Phoenix 85004 602/252-4804
**Arkansas Bar Assn.*	C. E. Ransick 400 W. Markham Little Rock 72201 501/375-4605
State Bar of California	John S. Malone 601 McAllister St. San Francisco 94102 415/922-1440

From Martindale-Hubbell national lawyers directory

Colorado Bar Assn.   William B. Miller
                                    200 W. 14th Ave.
                                    Denver 80204
                                    303/222-9421

Connecticut Bar Assn.   Daniel Hovey
                                    15 Lewis St.
                                    Hartford 06103
                                    203/249-9141

Delaware State Bar Assn.   Jan M. S. Black
                                    P.O. Box 1328
                                    Wilmington 19899
                                    302/658-5102

*District of Columbia Bar   R. Patrick Maxwell
                                    Ste. 840
                                    1426 H St., N.W.
                                    Washington 20005
                                    202/638-1500

Bar Assn. of the   Marie J. Rivera
    District of Columbia   1819 H St., N.W.
                                    Washington 20006
                                    202/223-1480

*The Florida Bar   Marshall R. Cassedy
                                    The Florida Bar Ctr.
                                    Tallahassee 32304
                                    904/222-5286

*State Bar of Georgia   Richard Bell
                                    1510 Fulton Nat. Bk. Bldg.
                                    Atlanta 30303
                                    404/522-6255

Hawaii State Bar Assn.   Eleanor I. Pierce
                                    P.O. Box 26
                                    Honolulu 96810
                                    808/537-1868

*Idaho State Bar

Ronald L. Kull
P.O. Box 895
Boise 83701
208/342-8958

Illinois State Bar Assn.

John H. Dickason
Illinois Bar Ctr.
Springfield 62701
217/525-1760

Indiana State Bar Assn.

Jack Lyle
230 E. Ohio St.
Indianapolis 46204
317/639-5465

Iowa State Bar Assn.

Edward H. Jones
1101 Fleming Bldg.
Des Moines 50309
515/243-3179

Kansas Bar Assn.

Ken Klein
P.O. Box 1037
Topeka 66601
913/234-5696

*Kentucky Bar Assn.

Leslie G. Whitmer
315 W. Main St.
Frankfort 40601
502/564-3795

*Louisiana State Bar
   Assn.

Thomas O. Collins, Jr.
Rm. 101
301 Loyola Ave.
New Orleans 70112
504/522-9172

Maine State Bar Assn.

Edward M. Bonney
P.O. Box 788
Augusta 04330
207/622-7523

Maryland State Bar Assn.	Arthur L. Mullen, Jr. 905 Keyser Bldg. Baltimore 21202 301/685-7878
Massachusetts Bar Assn.	Carl A. Modecki One Center Plaza Boston 02108 617/523-4529
*State Bar of Michigan	Michael Franck 306 Townsend St. Lansing 48933 517/372-9030
Minnesota State Bar Assn.	Gerald A. Regnier 100 Minnesota Fed. Bldg. Minneapolis 55402 612/335-1183
*Mississippi State Bar	George H. Van Zant P.O. Box 1032 Jackson 39205 601/948-4471
*The Missouri Bar	Wade F. Baker P.O. Box 119 Jefferson City 65101 314/635-4128
State Bar of Montana	Kent M. Parcell P.O. Box 4669 Helena 59601 406/4422-7660
*Nebraska State Bar Assn.	1019 Sharp Bldg. Lincoln 68508 402/475-7091

State Bar of Nevada   Maurice J. Sullivan
P.O. Box 2125
Reno 89505
702/323-0338

New Hampshire Bar Assn.   Joseph S. Hayden
77 Market St.
Manchester 03101
603/669-4869

New Jersey State Bar
  Assn.   Dalton W. Menhall
172 W. State St.
Trenton 08608
609/394-1101

State Bar of New Mexico   Celene Greene
1117 Stanford, N.E.
Albuquerque 87131
505/842-3063

New York State Bar Assn.   John E. Berry
One Elk St.
Albany 12207
518/445-1211

North Carolina State Bar   B. E. James
P.O. Box 25850
Raleigh 27611
919/828-4620

North Carolina Bar Assn.   William M. Storey
1025 Wade Ave.
Raleigh 27605
919/828-0561

State Bar Assn.
  North Dakota   Robert P. Schuller
118 N. 3rd St.
Bismarck 58501
701/255-1404

State Bar Assn.
  Ohio   Joseph B. Miller
33 West Eleventh Ave.
Columbus 43201
614/421-2121

*Oklahoma Bar Assn.

J. Dwain Schmidt
P.O. Box 53036
Oklahoma City 73105
405/524-2365

*Oregon State Bar

John H. Holloway
1776 S.W. Madison Ave.
Portland 97205
503/229-5788

Pennsylvania Bar Assn.

Frederick H. Bolton
Pennsylvania Bar Ctr.
P.O. Box 186
Harrisburg 17108
717/238-6715

*Bar Assn. of Puerto Rico

Osvaldo R. Gian Chini
Apartado 1900
San Juan 00903
809/724-3358

*Rhode Island Bar Assn.

Edward P. Smith
1804 Industrial Bk. Bldg.
Providence 02903
401/421-5740

South Carolina Bar Assn.

Robert N. DuRant
P.O. Box 11297
Columbia 29211
803/799-6653

*State Bar of South Dakota

William K. Sahr
222 E. Capitol
Pierre 57501
605/224-7554

Tennessee Bar Assn.

Billie R. Bethel
1717 W. End Ave.
Nashville 37203
615/329-1601

State Bar of Texas	H. C. Pittman Capitol Station P.O. Box 12487 Austin 78711 512/476-6823
Utah State Bar	Dean W. Sheffield 425 E. First South Salt Lake City 84101 801/322-1015
Vermont Bar Assn.	Beth Goodrich P.O. Box 100 Montpelier 05602 802/223-2020
Virginia State Bar	N. Samuel Clifton 700 E. Main St. Richmond 23219 804/786-2061
Virginia Bar Assn.	A. Ward Sims P.O. Box 5206 Charlottesville 22903 804/977-1396
*Washington State Bar Assn.	G. Edward Friar 505 Madison Seattle 98104 206/622-6054
*West Virginia State Bar	Duke Nordlinger Stern E-404, State Capitol Charleston 25305 304/346-8414
West Virginia Bar Assn.	F. Witcher McCullough P.O. Box 346 Charleston 25322 304/342-1474

State Bar of Wisconsin   James E. Hough
402 W. Wilson
Madison 53703
608/257-3838

Wyoming State Bar   George L. Simonton
1092 Sheridan Ave.
Cody 82414
307/587-5575

Index

239

CONDOR
BESTSELLERS

_____ **GAMES LAWYERS PLAY WITH YOUR MONEY**
by Blaine N. Simons
(Original Law) $2.25(018-8)

_____ **THE GREAT AMERICAN CRAZIES** by James Haskins with
Kathleen Benson and Ellen Inkelis
(Original Sociology) $1.95(014-5)

_____ **I AM MARY SHELLEY** by Barbara Lynne Devlin
(Original Occult) $1.95(007-2)

_____ **PORTRAITS OF CRIME** by Ector Garcia & Charles E. Pike
(Original Crime) $2.25(010-2)

_____ **RHODESIA** by Robin Moore
(Original Non-fiction) $2.25(005-6)

_____ **A SURVIVAL KIT FOR A HAPPIER MARRIAGE** by Sam Collins,
Jr., M.D.
(Psychology) $1.75(002-1)

_____ **THE WASHINGTON CONNECTION** by Robin Moore,
Lew Perdue with Nick Rowe
(Original Political Science) $2.25(004-8)

At your local bookstore or forward this coupon for ordering:

Condor Publishing Co., Inc.
Dept MO, 521 Fifth Ave., New York, N.Y. 10017
Please send me the Condor titles I have checked above. Enclosed is
$_____ (please add 50¢ to cover postage and handling). Send
check or money order—no cash or COD's. Order of 5 or more books
postage free.

Name _____

Address _____

City _____ State _____ Zip _____
Please allow at least 4 weeks for delivery.

CONDOR
BESTSELLERS

———— **THE LAZY MAN'S GUIDE TO PHYSICAL FITNESS** by Kenneth
D. Rose, M.D. & Jack Dies Martin
(Health & Physical Education) $1.75(012-9)

———— **GROWING UP HEALTHY** by Diego Redondo, M.D.
& Edith Freund
(Child Care) $1.75(008-0)

———— **THE GREAT TOMATO COOKBOOK** by Mike Michaelson
(Cookbook) $1.75(003-X)

———— **THE HAPPY HEART COOKBOOK** by Frayda Faigel, R.N.
(Original Cookbook) $1.95(011-0)

———— **RICE** by Betty L. Torre
(Original Cookbook) $1.95(017-X)

At your local bookstore or forward this coupon for
ordering:

Condor Publishing Co., Inc.

Dept MO, 521 Fifth Ave., New York, N.Y. 10017

Please send me the Condor titles I have checked above. Enclosed is
$_____ (please add 50¢ to cover postage and handling). Send
check or money order—no cash or COD's. Order of 5 or more books
postage free.

Name _____

Address _____

City _____ State _____ Zip _____

Please allow at least 4 weeks for delivery.

CONDOR
BESTSELLERS

_____THE CORRUPTORS by Gerald G. Griffin
(Original Suspense) $1.95(001-3)

_____OUR MISSILE'S MISSING by Robin Moore with
Stan Gebler Davies
(Original Suspense) $2.25(015-3)

_____THE POKER CLUB by Chet Cunningham
(Original Fiction) $2.25(013-7)

_____ROTUNDA by Robert R. Siegrist
(Original Suspense) $2.25(009-9)

_____THE STATUETTE by Jane Wald & Kathleen Wakefield
(Original Fiction) $1.95(006-4)

_____TERROR AT HILLCREST by Shannon Graham
(Original Law) $1.95(019-6)

At your local bookstore or forward this coupon
for ordering:

- - - - - - - - - - - - - - - - - - - -

Condor Publishing Co., Inc.
Dept MO, 521 Fifth Ave., New York, N.Y. 10017

Please send me the Condor titles I have checked above. Enclosed is
$ _____ (please add 50¢ to cover postage and handling). Send check
or money order—no cash or COD's. Order of 5 or more books postage free.

Name _____

Address _____

City _____ State _____ Zip _____
Please allow at least 4 weeks for delivery.

- - - - - - - - - - - - - - - - - - - -